Advance Praise for the PARDA Process: 5 Steps from Wishful Thinking to Sustained Change

Nancy Larson continues to be a trusted member of my Board of Advisors. I love the fact that she is now sharing her wisdom and process to those who seek out knowledge. The PARDA Process should be required for entrepreneurs and managers alike. Look at the process or problem intellectually–not just emotionally.

Leif Jensen, CPA
Leif Jensen and Associates

It is often said that life is difficult, yet many of the difficult parts are self-created by our own thinking. "The PARDA Process: 5 Steps from Wishful Thinking to Sustained Change" presents a clear, logical process for dealing with the issues and challenges one faces in life, whether simple or complex. Written in an easy-to-understand style that guides the reader through the thinking process, Dr. Larson presents true life examples of using (or not using) the PARDA Process that often hit home. This readable, well-written book will help anyone improve their way of thinking when dealing with life's issues or impending changes. I highly recommend it. In fact, I have already been talking and using it consciously for issues that cause one "Pause"...pun intended!

Robert C. Beiter, Ph.D., CCC-A
Audiologist and President
Forensic Audiologist Consultants, Inc.

This book describes the approach when faced with challenges that most of us know, but don't follow. By breaking down the steps Nancy has termed the "PARDA Process," it allows us to really stop and become our own therapist and advisor. This book is invaluable at the student as well as at the professional level to assess our goals and actions, so we can achieve the end result we desire. This book has taught me ways to handle life's challenges, and reminds us to ask for guidance from above.

Dr. Ann M. Collins, D.C.
Chiropractic Physician

The PARDA Process provides possibilities by using common sense, discerning prayer and a kinder, gentler life focus. Nancy's insights work across all lines: business, personal, and spiritual.

Luisa Buehler
Business Owner, Author and Christian

Knowing the author to be a skilled and untiring problem solver, I came to her book expecting a mystery. And, true to form, she has dared to delve that greatest of puzzles: how to build a life that approaches one's dreams. Drawing on a breadth of academic investigations, enhanced by her varied encounters as a counselor and librarian, she has packed the volume with practical wisdom and the tools within anyone's grasp to apply it.

Patricia Althen Cannon, Ph.D.
Former faculty of the Department of Library & Information
Studies
Northern Illinois University

The PARDA Process:
5 Steps from Wishful Thinking to Sustained Change

Nancy L. Larson, MLS, Ed.D.

Disclaimer

This book details the author's personal experiences with and opinions about strategic thinking and planning in order to achieve your goals. The author is not a licensed mental health or medical professional.

The author and publisher are providing this book and its contents on an "as is" basis and make no representations or warranties of any kind with respect to this book or its contents. The author and publisher disclaim all such representations and warranties, including, for example, warranties of merchantability and professional advice for a particular purpose. In addition, the author and publisher do not represent or warrant that the information accessible via this book is accurate, complete, or current.

The statements made about products and services have not been evaluated by the U.S. government. Please consult with your own legal or accounting professional regarding the suggestions and recommendations made in this book.

Except as specifically stated in this book, neither the author nor publisher, nor any authors, contributors, or other representatives will be liable for damages arising out of or in connection with the use of this book. This is a comprehensive limitation of liability that applies to all damages of any kind, including (without limitation) compensatory; direct, indirect or consequential damages; loss of data, income or profit; loss of or damage to property and claims of third parties.

You understand that this book is not intended as a substitute for consultation with a licensed medical, legal or accounting professional. Before you begin any change your lifestyle in any way, you will consult a licensed professional to ensure that you are doing what's best for your situation.

This book provides content related to strategic thinking and planning topics. As such, use of this book implies your acceptance of this disclaimer.

Depictions of events or individuals in this book have been altered or changed to protect people's privacy. Any resemblance to actual persons (living or dead) is purely coincidental.

Dedicated to Ron, my beloved Viking

Jag älskar dig

Song of Solomon 8:6

But the goal of our instruction is love from a pure heart

and a good conscience and a sincere faith.

I Timothy 1:5 (NASB)

Table of Contents

Part I

Laying the Foundation: What Works?

My disillusionment with counseling and psychotherapy began before I finished graduate school when I strode into my dissertation advisor's office.

"Look at these books," I said. *"House of Cards: The Myth of Psychotherapy* by Robin Dawes. *What We Can Change and What We Can't: And the Wisdom to Know the Difference* by Martin Seligman. I came across these two articles showing there's no statistical difference in improvement for patients who receive therapy from a Ph.D. psychologist versus a college student with six weeks of training. The lack of improvement in the control group wasn't insignificant, either." I glared at him, demanding answers.

Dr. James sat in elegant, sartorial splendor complete with tailored suit and styled hair. He looked more like the managing director of a British firm than a rumpled American academic. He was never called "Dr. Jim"; he was always "Dr. James."

Distraught doctoral students were nothing new to him. Steepling his long fingers, his next words shocked me.

"You're right. Much of psychotherapy doesn't work. Most clinicians figure it out roughly eighteen months after graduation. You're ahead of the curve." His calmness unnerved me.

"But, but, but, how do you still teach classes if you don't believe in this? And now what am I going to do?"

Frantic, I realized I had invested several hundred hours in writing and research on the dissertation itself, let alone the years of classroom study toward my degree.

I struggled not to think about the money I had wasted. Many people don't finish their doctoral dissertation and have the dreaded letters "ABD" (All But Dissertation) after their name for years. I vowed I wouldn't be one of them.

Still, when I spoke, I felt my time, money, and work crumble around me. I struggled not to judge, but his hypocrisy shocked me. He shrugged.

"That's why I've shifted to teaching transpersonal psychology. Your dissertation—that's up to you." He picked up a few papers, signaling our meeting was over.

Two-thirds of my dissertation was done, and I didn't want to waste years of work. So, I finished up and continued to teach the basic counseling skills courses because, if nothing else, they helped when relating to clients, friends, and family.

Dr. James's words haunted me. He had two doctorates, taught graduate courses, worked in the counseling field, and told me outright that psychotherapy didn't work. I kept circling back to the same thoughts. If what he'd said were true, then I had wasted several years and thousands of dollars. Now what?

In all good conscience, could I be a therapist, knowing what I knew?

In addition to my doctorate, I was one class short of a second master's degree in library science that I'd started while working on my dissertation. The research skills I learned were valuable. Unfortunately, being a librarian didn't pay as much as counseling, and jobs were hard to find. After my encounter with Dr. James, however, I needed to redefine my future.

The Real Education Comes After School

Between semesters and job searches, I worked for temp agencies that sent me to a host of companies. Law firms. Insurance. Technology. Pharmaceuticals. A wine distributor. What an eye-opener. While I knew I didn't fit in corporate America, the temp jobs paid the bills, and I experienced a variety of company cultures and employees. Some jobs ended in a few days, while others lasted weeks. Wherever I went, I had to learn the ropes in a hurry and think on my feet. It was exhausting, but my background had taught me to listen and empathize with stressed coworkers.

After several false starts, I found a full-time job working with disabled and home-bound library patrons in addition to the usual reference services. The position related to my degrees, was close to home and offered health coverage. Most of all, I realized I loved being around books. Of course, I never had enough time to read everything that caught my eye.

During the next two decades, most of my jobs were with non-profits except for several years as a business writer and analyst. Having worked at so many places, I felt like a business anthropologist. Most of the organizations were secular, while a few defined themselves as openly Christian.

Regardless of whether secular or religious, people were the same. Everyone had problems and sought practical, easy solutions. Most had no idea where to start untangling the messes in their lives. Worse, many problems were through no fault of their own.

Problem-solving Skills

When I worked as a counselor and therapist, I discovered that most of my clients needed strategies that combined both thinking and action but also respected their emotions. They seldom had a clue how to think for themselves, and they expected someone to hand them answers with no effort on their part. No one took the time to teach problem-solving skills, rather than constantly relying on someone else for help.

While it would have been great to have clients "cured," I felt it was most important they become empowered to make better decisions. Plus, there's seldom a quick fix. Events had occurred in the past, but the consequences remained.

Let's be clear: I'm all for counseling, especially for painful situations. Our lives challenge us, but most of us don't need months of therapy to face our difficulties. I struggled to figure out a straightforward process folks could use when they got stuck.

My clients—and everyone else—want to know how to magically fix problems in their lives. But I can't wave my wand and have them awaken next morning, situation solved. When one problem ended, another would pop up. I guess you can take this woman out of the counseling profession, but my training, experience, and caring remain indefinitely.

After I cut my ties to the counseling profession and became a full-time librarian and freelance writer, I kept running into people who wailed, "But I don't know what to *do!*" Like my former clients, they wanted me to do their thinking for them and hand them a map. I felt helpless and irritated, because I no longer wanted to spend hours problem-solving. How could I provide solutions that allowed people to think and do their own work?

I kept asking, "What works? What is your next step?"

Many patrons who came to the library had lost their jobs. What should they do next? Where do they learn multiple computer applications in six weeks and create a résumé? In addition, my coworkers and I fielded questions such as these:

Patron: "I've been diagnosed with cancer. Do you have a book or DVD?"
Librarian: "Let me show you items in the 600s, and some articles, too."
Patron: "My marriage is falling apart because my husband watches porn. What should I do?"
Librarian: "Try the 150s, self-help, and 646, relationships."
Patron: "Where's the nearest food pantry?"
Librarian: "Here's a list of local agencies for you."
Patron: "Where should my kid go to college, if at all?"
Librarian: "See the 370s for books about education."

If these responses sound flippant, they're not. Increasingly, librarians are *de facto* social workers helping the mentally ill, unemployed, and homeless. With ongoing drastic cuts in social services, people are turning to local libraries in droves. I never thought I would draw on my previous training to deal with issues such as unemployment and job training, let alone drug and alcohol addiction.

This was *not* what I expected in solid, middle-class suburbia.

Where Do People Learn to Think?

The more I thought about it, the more I wondered: "How do some people learn to think effectively by asking questions and plug away until they find answers, while others give up?" I don't blame educators, knowing they work long hours with limited resources. And parents? If they haven't learned this skill themselves, how can they teach their kids?

It's fine to ask for assistance, to reach out to friends and professionals who have the information you lack. My complaint centers on people who don't take even a few minutes to think about their problem or try to identify ideas. They frantically call their buddies, locate dozens of contradictory solutions from the internet, and still have no plan or strategy for what to do. Or worse, people make suggestions, only to be told, "That's too hard." "That's a lot of work." "I can't do that." Friends and families have told them repeatedly they need to do something—and they can't.

"Don't bother people for help without first trying to solve the problem yourself." – Colin Powell

I've had to help adults learn everything from how to read maps and bus schedules to creating budgets and write step-by-step plans for work projects. Along with asking questions and exploring ideas, another missing life skill is critical thinking. With access to the internet, I'm staggered by the volume of information available:

- College-level courses.
- Medical information.
- Cute animal videos.

- How-to web sites.
- The latest trends and news.
- And much more.

There's a computer programming expression, "Garbage in, garbage out." Today, if information comes from a computer, it's "garbage in, gospel truth out." When people find something online, they assume it's accurate. They protest: "You mean I can't use Wikipedia? I heard they edit all the time."

My questions became, "How do we teach people to assess the accuracy and validity of what they find?" "Why can't they think for themselves, instead of running to the internet, their friends, or the store clerk with their problems?" How can I empower them?

From this place, I state my conclusions:

- Insight doesn't produce change.
- Willpower doesn't work for long.
- Change doesn't happen easily.
- Permanent change takes time—if it ever happens.
- There are no easy solutions.
- There's no guarantee any solution will always work.
- Life consists of one problem after another.
- It's hard to balance feelings versus thinking.

Does Anything Work?

Many self-help books, whether religious or secular, offer excellent advice for Christians and nonbelievers alike. But when I began reading them, the suggestions were all different or contradictory. The processes were too complicated, so I'd give up. Initially, people were enthusiastic about achieving their goals, but then their brains figured they'd had enough affirmations and visualizations. "I've already done the work, I feel virtuous, and I'll start tomorrow...."

By the way, you'll see in this book that positive thinking isn't as helpful as once thought. Furthermore, it *negatively* affects our economy, according to researchers led by A. Timur Sevincer of the University of Hamburg and Gabriele Oettingen of New York University.[1]

At home one day, I pulled all my self-help books and stacked them in piles. I was searching for answers to the question, "How do I figure out what works and what doesn't?" Here's what I observed:

- We try to figure out a situation, and we can't.
- The Bible doesn't have answers to our specific problem.
- The issue(s) seems insurmountable.
- Where do we start, let alone envision the next step?
- There's no strategy for workable, long-term solutions.
- We vacillate between frantic action and inertia.

When I stared at the stacks, I wondered if long-term change is ever achievable without years of therapy. In lieu of therapy, I wanted ideas that would:

- Be easy to use and remember.
- Balance action and thinking.
- Be acceptable to Christians and nonbelievers alike.
- Kick in automatically when under pressure.
- Useful for solving problems and changing habits.
- Get us started when we're paralyzed into inactivity.
- Honor our compassion, emotions, and thoughts.
- *Avoid reliance solely on emotions or willpower.*

The last statement felt like the crux of the issue. Almost everything I've studied about solving problems and creating change seemed to require willpower. Determination. Gritting one's teeth and getting it done, come what may. I don't know about you, but my strength and grit dissolve before breakfast. Waves of enthusiasm get me started but dissipate an hour later. No wonder the practices of visualization and affirmations are popular. Real problem-solving and change both require demanding work.

This spurred me to find a process that allowed people choices in solving their everyday problems. By whittling down the smaller problem branches, larger ones become easier.

Ongoing Challenges

While we experience the death of loved ones, ill-health, unemployment, and more, most of the time it's the ongoing daily challenges that frustrate us. Playwright Anton Chekhov said, "Any idiot can face a crisis—it's day-to-day living that wears you out." Amen, brother. I've searched for answers for years. Unfortunately, quick fixes remain elusive. Making changes, creating new habits, and solving problems take time, which we complain we don't have or it's too complicated. We give up in weariness and/or frustration.

Gandhi once said, "Strength does not come from physical capacity. It comes from an indomitable will." Unlike Gandhi, I don't have a strong will.

Can We Change?

If willpower doesn't work, what does?

For years, professionals such as psychologist James Prochaska, author of *Changing for Good,* have studied how people change. They're seldom successful on the first try. People need to think about change, identify the steps, then try, try again. This applies to diets, smoking, or changing any kind of habit.

Furthermore, no one can "make" you change. Telling someone to lose weight or stop drinking because you love them, is doomed to failure. Similarly, internal pressure to change because you "should" won't work either.

Complicating matters, advertisers, fast food restaurants, and shopping mall owners use scientific findings to ensure their customers spend money and consume their products. Fast food is loaded with fat and sugar to stimulate cravings. Stores are designed so shoppers don't have a straight path to the door.

Instead, they must meander through racks of attractive clothes and shelves of gadgets. Television blasts images of gorgeous people touting their wares, implying that if you buy their product, you too, will be rich, beautiful, and successful.

Being realistic about change requires taking small steps, examining what did or didn't work, and trying again—and again. It means dealing with the emotional components of self-condemnation, doubt, and maybe despair.

God, who works on our hearts and minds, makes us "new creations" in Christ, meaning "the old has passed away" (II Corinthians 5:17). He doesn't do this immediately in our lives (oh how I wish), but He refines and shapes us to His image over time.

Problems, Habits, and Sustained Change

Certain changes can't be sustained, and you set yourself up for failure when you try. For me to become more organized, for example, is an ongoing struggle no matter how hard I push. Yet looking back at the changes I've made, I find papers faster and there's less clutter. I'll never be one of those mavens who publish bestsellers on getting organized, but I usually find my documents when I need them. I'm okay with imperfection.

Struggling to always become better has ever-diminishing returns. It makes me (and others) ask, "Do I keep going or choose to be at peace, believing I've done the best I can?"

Women have come to me and said things like, "I wish I could be more outgoing like my friend Rena. She talks to anyone, and I stand there like a doofus." Of course, you can learn social skills (and it's helpful to do so), but if you don't enjoy going to parties on Saturday night, then why do you push against your temperament again and again? Why make yourself miserable because you can't change who you are?

I saw an awful lot of people around me who worked hard but didn't see results. I wondered what to do when they came to me in tears of anger and frustration. I found myself listening to people struggle and told them point-blank I had no answers. I could, however, sit with them, and together we could explore small steps and actions. I tried to "rejoice with those who rejoice and weep with those who weep." (Romans 12:15)

Others attempted to change but lacked the knowledge or skills to carry out their decisions. While they thought it was lack of willpower, I could observe gaps in their strategies. Their problems seemed to fall into two categories: immediate and ongoing. When the toilet overflows, we clean up the mess and call a plumber to figure out the cause. The steps are clear, and the fix itself is straightforward.

Then there are ongoing issues, such as complicated relationships or stubborn habits that refuse to yield to change. Our minds run in circles. We ask for advice and search online. Worse, we think we've dealt with the situation, but it recurs again and again despite our best efforts. How do we cope with a disabled child who will never get better or a spouse's chronic depression?

A Framework for Change and Problem-Solving

By applying the PARDA Process, I started seeing answers to all the questions I'd been asking that would help me—and help others. It's a problem-solving tool to use as needed and works at whittling at stubborn issues instead of attacking them with a sledge hammer. Changing habits isn't easy, but the PARDA Process simplifies the process and helps maintain the change.

This is a framework that enables you to step back from your tangled emotions so your brain functions more clearly. It hears the emotions from the heart then allows the brain to gather information and devise solutions. The war between head and heart begins to heal, and the two ways of perceiving start working in tandem.

However, it takes time to learn new thought patterns and avoid slipping back into old habits. When we stumble, the PARDA Process contains tools that identify the cause and get us on track toward sustained change. By taking time and being gentle with ourselves, we lower our stress and stop beating ourselves up.

The PARDA Process was distilled from years of trial and error. In developing it, I learned what worked from clients, friends, families, and my own life. Today I continue try to discern what to do versus following a patchwork of Bible verses. I'm still learning, heaven knows, with the difference being I now have a framework to help me. My life's journey has been challenged by the PARDA Process because it forced me to become more honest about what I was thinking and feeling. That isn't always pleasant.

The statement "God helps those who help themselves" is not in the Bible but is attributed to Benjamin Franklin. The Bible says to use the gifts and talents God has given us but also in submission to Him. Total self-reliance and self-righteousness are a slap to Jesus Christ, who said, "If anyone desires to come after Me, let him deny himself, and take up his cross, and follow Me." Matthew 16:24 (NKJV)

While I had good intentions, I realized the best I could offer to those seeking help and who didn't want a "religious" answer, was giving them a way to work through their problems. They had to stop beating themselves up, sort through their emotions without denying them, and figure out an action plan.

My experiences in the business world plus my counseling background made me realize we must do two things:

- Balance our emotional desire to change and
- Devise strategies that create the least amount of struggle.

All of this resulted in developing the PARDA Process.

Two Secret Weapons

My two secret weapons are *writing dumps* and *micromoves*, which are explored in detail in this book.

Writing dumps and rants allow you to spill onto paper all the messy thoughts and feelings in your head and then detach from the upset while you examine what you wrote.

Micromoves are minor changes you choose to make consistently in order to create change or develop new habits. The secret is to make them so miniscule and gradual that your mind and emotions don't fight the change. In fact, the smaller the better. You are in control.

A reporter once asked the poet Robert Frost if he had a philosophy of life. Frost paused. "I can summarize it in three words," he said. "Life goes on."

Frost was right. We cling to delightful times and wish unpleasant experiences would go away. You'll find applying the PARDA Process is useful for all your life's experiences—both delightful and unpleasant so you can move on instead of clinging to events and emotions.

Life will move on, whether you want it to or not, so I encourage you to play. Explore. Have fun. Be present in your life. The PARDA Process helps you achieve that when you're willing to give it a chance.

Where is God in All of This?

People who know me ask why I don't present a gospel-centered message about God's love and how He works in people's lives. Depending on where I'm working, talking about spiritual things is taboo.

Being a Christian, I've tried to make sense of it all. When I worked for religious organizations, I realized my employers assumed that their employees have a personal spiritual life. Just as scriptural principles guided their organization's goals, they believed God would provide clear answers to their employees' problems.

I struggle with doubt and hate admitting to it. Why, oh why couldn't I be like other Christians I know, happy to describe all the wonderful things God was doing in their lives? Why couldn't I have a life like a sterling Facebook profile: gleaming, polished, and best of all, problem-free? Did others wonder, too? Or was it only me?

Many believers project a cheerful, perky personality that made me feel inferior. When I got to know them—whether at work or church—they revealed their pain and doubt.

"You are a God who hides Himself" (Isaiah 45:15) seems to define my relationship with Him. I walk by faith and not by sight, trusting He will give me what I need. Looking back, I see how He has been present every step of the way, loving and carrying me through my ups and downs. He will never leave me nor forsake me (Deuteronomy 31:8; Hebrews 13:5), but that doesn't mean I'm always happy.

I Resign

Despite my disillusionment with counseling and therapy, people kept coming to me for help. In my roles as therapist and now as a librarian, I learned people would love to have someone hand them answers on a platter.

Unfortunately, life doesn't work that way. The PARDA Process, while it arose out of a dream, is my attempt to reconcile the tension of walking by faith versus working at change. It offers a way for folks to work on their lives and resolve problems on their own, along with asking God and others for help.

For myself, I needed to set boundaries, yet I hated leaving hurting people in the lurch. No one had taught them how to think. The wonderful thing about being a reference librarian is that I can offer lots of materials, but it's up to the individual to make the effort. Changing habits or working on relationships is hard, but I refuse to rescue people any longer.

If it's a significant issue such as depression, addiction, or abuse, seek professional help. Otherwise, stop shopping around for advice on the internet or from well-meaning friends. Instead, take responsibility and identify what you need to do. Once you have thought through your challenge, then ask for assistance.

Real change, however, takes place on the spiritual level. What do you do when you receive a life-threatening diagnosis? Deal with a marriage break-up or loss of a job with little hope of finding one with a salary close to the one you made before? How do you cope with the inevitable tough times?

If you're offended by my including God or Jesus Christ in this book, ignore the religious content and read anyway. The PARDA Process itself works without a spiritual component. Frankly, I struggled whether to include my beliefs and relationship with Jesus Christ along with the PARDA Process. I felt compelled to do so because I saw changes in my own spiritual life while I wrote this book.

Consequently, I wove the biblical principles and verses into my writing. If you take pride in being intellectually honest, be willing to be open. I must trust that, just as I am honest with my readers, they will be open in return. What do you have to lose? Your life hasn't been a bowl of cherries and neither has mine. When my world is turned upside down—when nothing makes sense—all I do is cling to the Lord Jesus Christ in trust that He knows what's best. This has been a challenge, but the richness and depth God has added to my life is incalculable. Christianity is not about self-improvement, but about our brokenness before a holy, loving God. The basics of faith are found in the verses listed in Appendix A.

According to one account (possibly apocryphal), an atheist visiting Martin Buber, a rabbi and philosopher, demanded he prove the existence of God. Buber refused, and the atheist left feeling angry. But as he left, Buber called after him, "But can you be *sure* there is no God?" Reportedly, the atheist claimed the question haunted him for forty years.

Or what about Jim Elliot, a missionary martyred for his faith? He said, "He is no fool who gives what he cannot keep to gain what he cannot lose." Ultimately, we lose all that we have whether we want to or not when we die.

If you don't want to step out in faith to trust God, I hope you still make sensible, wise decisions. I turn to the PARDA Process because it allows me to rely upon God and retain my personal responsibility. It buys time by letting me choose what I think, speak, and believe, especially when under stress. It has become an ongoing resource for sustained change. That's why I recommend these simple steps to carry with you and use when needed.

How to Use This Book

To enable you to get the most out of the ideas in this book, I start with Laying the Foundation, about my disillusionment with traditional psychotherapy. Following that, Chapter 1 explores how the PARDA Process was created and why it's useful.

Chapters 2 through 8 explore the five steps of the PARDA Process: **Pause, Acknowledge, Reflect, Decide,** and **Act**. These words are shown in bold throughout, so you see how the individual steps flow together. Following this step-by-step process keeps you from rushing into problem-solving then wondering why it all went wrong. Doing the steps in sequence produces the best results.

Chapters 7 and 8—**Decide** and **Act**—include tools I've discovered to help you make decisions and carry out your steps. Chapter 9 takes this further by exploring several ACTion Tools to get you moving once you've thought and felt things out. Chapter 10 elaborates on the concept of Micromoves, the small steps needed to shake loose problems and habits.

You can build on your new habits by picking up the pace—what I call Ramp-ups in Chapter 11. I challenge our assumptions about the law of attraction and positive thinking in Chapter 12, while Chapter 13 explores ways moving on in your life. The examples are conversations incorporating the PARDA Process, but for the best results, you'll see why I strongly urge folks to make brief notes.

Part II shows how to use the PARDA Process on several issues. While you read this book, you'll find endless topics of your own to work on.

Start by reading or skimming through the book once to understand the overall flow, then go back and reread. Use a notebook and take notes to make the PARDA Process your own.

I've included stories of people I've met and how they successfully used the PARDA Process to solve their challenges. I share my own struggles as well because I'm a work in progress. Names and details have been changed to protect people's privacy. In some instances, I've combined several examples into one story for clarity. The exceptions are when I relate my own experiences. In some instances, however, I've changed details to protect friends and family.

The goal of the PARDA Process is to get people to think for themselves and identify ways to move out of being stuck. It also alleviates emotional upheaval. You'll see what I've learned and how it has helped me and others.

Chapter 1

What is the PARDA Process?

After years of struggle to find quick, effortless ways to help people solve their own problems, I awoke one morning with five words running through my sleepy brain. To stop them from endlessly repeating, I wrote them down: **Pause**, **Acknowledge**, **Reflect**, **Decide**, **Act**. Then I went about my day.

A few days later, the words came again, more insistently. I wrote the words down again, this time including a few disjointed thoughts. To my amazement, the concepts seemed to work. I realized I had been using these steps for years, but until now, I had never pulled them together. The PARDA Process was born.

Initially, I didn't believe this would work. Ever the perpetual graduate student, I pored through academic journals and read books. Slowly, I began to see the steps had validity and could be applied in a variety of situations.

During graduate school, I learned that a solid, practical theory must enable you to back yourself out of a situation with a client when you get stuck. This is what the PARDA Process does. When you **Pause** for two or three breaths, you give yourself space. You think about what happened and make choices. This slows you down long enough to enable you to see what's happening in the moment. If you can't do anything about it now, come back later and reflect on what happened

Pause. Stop for a few seconds and take one breath. Or two breaths. Or a couple more, if possible. If nothing else, this will stop you from saying or doing something you'll regret later. Call out a quick prayer to God for peace and calm. Gently hold your feelings.

Acknowledge. Accept what you are thinking and feeling in the moment, no matter how distasteful or unpleasant. Continue to be with your emotions, cradling them without judgment. Be in a safe place and verbalize those thoughts of wanting to rip out someone's hair or trash their flower garden. Write down your thoughts, leaving in the spelling errors and grammatical mistakes. Allow your pulse to slow down and the flush to leave your face. Stop trying to pretty up undesirable thoughts. Christians and non-believers alike are ashamed to admit they get angry and not act like nice people.

Next, spell out all your frustrations about your poor choices and the shame that comes with them. I find myself confessing to God, saying, "I screwed up. I made a mistake. I'll clean up my mess." In my family I was raised to solve my own problems and not bother anyone for help. That's why it's taken me years to say, "God, I messed up. Please help me."

It's an ongoing challenge, and I've learned through experience I can't do it on my own.

King David, who was called "a man after God's own heart," wrote what commentators label "imprecatory psalms. He wished all sorts of evil upon his enemies. "Let his days be few, *And* let another take his office. Let his children be fatherless, And his wife a widow...." Psalm 109, verses 8-12 (NKJV, italics in the original)

These verses contradict the commands of Jesus to "love your enemies and do good." (Luke 6:35)

When I'm honest, I identify with King David in his angry moments, and these verses speak to my heart. I must ask God for the ability to bless my enemies when I fantasize about torturing them with a thousand paper cuts. I suggest you resist the temptation to bury your "not nice" feelings. Instead, swap the burial desire for genuine curiosity and self-examination.

It's okay to be uncomfortable, including in God's presence. Psalm 139 reminds us that He knows us intimately and our innermost thoughts.

Reflect. Is what you are saying to yourself accurate in this situation? Or are your emotions running high and affecting your thoughts and actions? God's word says, "There's no temptation [trial] taking you, but such as is common to man." (2 Corinthians

5:17) Or how about Ecclesiastes 1:9? "There's nothing new under the sun," says the writer of the book, who is thought to be David's son Solomon but is usually named as Prophet or Teacher in these verses.

David came before the Lord to confess his sins regarding his affair with Bathsheba and the murder of her husband. He came knowing what he had done was wrong. He didn't blame anyone else, nor did he whitewash his actions. (Psalm 51).

When we **Reflect**, it's not the time or place to pass judgment on ourselves. We admit what we're experiencing in all its ugliness, then we step back and ask for God's help and guidance in the situation.

I tell others to *be gentle* with themselves. In fact, I repeat it over and over because we forget to be as kind to ourselves as we are to our friends. We beat ourselves up. (More about this later when we explore the concept of self-compassion.) A useful emotion is curiosity instead of condemnation. Ask questions with an open mind. What started the chain of events? What mood was I in? What will I do differently next time?

Decide. You have already paused, acknowledged, and reflected what's happening in the moment. Now, how will you move forward? What will you do next? What choices will you make? Are these choices in line with biblical principles, or do you think they're skirting an edge?

Perhaps there are no specific answers from Scriptures for your exact situation. There are, however, guidelines in terms of acting with integrity. For a reality check if you need it, discuss your situation with people whose judgment you respect and trust.

Act. Once you have made up your mind, then act on your decision by taking small moves. What miniscule next step or steps will you take? How will you know when the situation is resolved? What benchmarks will you use to avoid spinning your wheels? What small step is calling you first?

Next, do a fast recheck on the quality of your decision, then go for it. The tiniest steps count—the "micromoves" featured in Chapter 9.

As you become familiar with the steps, you'll work through them with speed and ease. Pausing a moment or two will be enough (if you let it) to keep you from making a wrong move.

By exploring each section, you'll design a series of steps meant to tailor your efforts for maximum effect. That way, you have choices to explore what works best for you.

Benefits of the PARDA Process

The PARDA Process is simple and easy to use. If you are willing commit to the steps over time, it can produce dramatic results. Taking the process slowly lets you to build habits and sustain meaningful changes.

When I thought about change, I realized that first I had to commit to one goal at a time. Second, I had to keep it both simple and specific. Third, if I wanted to change, I knew it would have to take time. Finally, I realized I needed a plan to make the necessary changes. I've watched so many friends, family, and clients struggle to sustain change. I wanted to be realistic about how to maintain their choices.

Most people fall into two groups: 1) those who create logical, elaborate strategies but become paralyzed and can't move forward, and 2) those who take what their hearts and guts say and charge ahead but have few plans. One approach isn't worse than the other. But if one's mind and heart work in tandem, life runs smoother. Rather than relying on one modality, I suggest it's better to flex between one approach or the other and generate multiple ideas.

The challenge is to figure out which mindset works with which individuals or team. How do the analytical thinkers get a move on? How do you make the enthusiastic "full-speed-ahead" types take five minutes to evaluate and plan? This is where the PARDA Process comes in. Because it balances thought and action, both groups benefit. You find solutions to problems without spending days thinking or rushing ahead in wasted activity. Generate ideas to spur both groups toward change.

What's the Big Deal About Writing It Down?

Along with being playful, gentle, and taking small steps, write down your thoughts instead of putting them in your device. Getting them out of your head and on paper shifts the problem and offers distance from it.

Most of the time, when I work with individuals, we can talk through the process, and we're done—until the next crisis. By doing the steps on paper, however, people develop their own strategies and create change.

At this time, take several sheets of paper, a pen, and a timer set to fifteen or twenty minutes and write about something bugging you right now. And write more. Include the four-letter words, bad grammar, and rotten spelling. If you get stuck, repeat the last word(s) and keep going until the timer dings.

Whatever you do, don't stop until the timer tells you your time is up. Important: Resist the temptation to sneak a look at Facebook, emails, or other distraction(s).

Folks fight me tooth and nail about writing because they resist writing by hand. Yet its effectiveness is backed by scientific research. A number of consultants and trainers who teach business leaders now insist their participants write by hand—at least during the seminars. Many participants, however, continue the practice once the requirement is removed.

People ask me if writing on a computer is as effective as writing by hand. My answer is that powerful neurological changes take place while writing in detail about painful events. Using pen and paper reduces the temptation to avoid topics by checking social media or email "for just a minute." Before you know it, your planned writing time has vanished.

We all make choices. I see dedicated musicians practicing for hours. Swimmers immerse themselves in frigid water early in the morning. What do you choose to commit to?

"Writing things down is the first step toward making it happen." – Lee Iacocca

Science supports the value of writing. Social psychologist James Pennebaker, in his book *Writing to Heal: A Guided Journal for Recovering from Trauma and Emotional Upheaval*, explored the concept of "therapeutic writing." According to his research, focused writing about a traumatic event for as few as four days can bring about substantial emotional healing. He encourages people to explore painful events with their effects in detail for twenty minutes without stopping. Pennebaker makes it clear this is different than keeping a diary. Furthermore, he warns that endless writing does not replace action, nor is it an excuse for endless complaining.

Writing by hand slows down the brain long enough to make thoughts accessible. It eliminates the temptation to delve into distractions. Writing instead of typing reduces the temptation to self-edit or correct spelling and grammar. There is evidence that writing by hand activates various parts of the brain by creating more of an emotional "punch" compared to using an electronic device. This is true because when we search inside for the right words to describe our experiences and emotions, we deepen and sharpen our awareness. Our repertoire of descriptive words develops shades of meaning we didn't realize before.

My skills are superb, and I can type 60+ WPM for hours. Yes, I can get a lot out—but when I write by hand, my attention is focused and it's harder to evade my thoughts and emotions. I wish I had a better way, but I've learned that writing by hand is powerful.

People tell me their handwriting is awful, they can't spell, and their grammar is atrocious. I reassure them by saying no one will see their sloppy handwriting because it's for their eyes only. And because they're the ones reading it and no one else, they don't have to worry about spelling and grammar.

"But it takes too long." Again, there are distinct advantages of writing by hand for greater accessibility and the activation of various parts of the brain. By starting with shorter entries, you just might find the writing process so rewarding that you're willing to make more time. And I'm not suggesting hours, either. Depending upon the situation, 10 minutes or so daily or every few days is more than enough, except when you want to dig deeper.

Pam Mueller of Princeton University and Daniel Oppenheimer of the University of California at UCLA sought to discover whether taking notes—either by hand or computer—affected learning.[2] Those who used computers had extensive notes but scored lower on tests than those who took notes by hand.

A similar study[3] conducted by faculty members at West Point with students taking a required economics class found comparable results. One group of students took notes by hand with no electronic devices, while a second group continued to take notes on their laptops. A third group could use their devices for taking class notes, but the tablets or laptops had to be flat on a table, so professors could see what they were typing. On the final exam, students who had written their notes by hand scored higher than those who used a tablet or laptop.

People challenge me with other complaints about the PARDA Process. I get it, but there's no shortcuts.

Practice Often

Use the PARDA Process for changing habits and meeting your goals. Struggling with what appears to be an impossible habit? Use the five steps to ponder your choices. If you can't seem to stop eating chips or watching too much TV, what tiny step would start a change? The PARDA Process appears deceptively simple. Don't be fooled. When used consistently, it generates results. Instead of becoming impatient and giving up—which is what got you into trouble in the first place—do something different. By taking it slow and then even slower, you build habits and sustain change over time.

"Rejoice in small things and they will continue to grow" – Slaven Vujic

I can guarantee that even with the best of intentions, you will have days where you can't do your small step. Or you skip it completely. You know what? Stuff happens. Forgive yourself quickly and get going. Something is always better than nothing.

Or, if you have a long-term goal that requires multiple steps, use this process to chunk things down. Identify what needs to be done and how you will cope with obstacles before they occur.

The PARDA Process is ideal for the irritating, everyday situations when we need to make decisions or when someone said something we can't put our finger on but feels off. It's helpful for sorting through a complex project or situation.

One caveat: While a quick fix during crises buys time, it's not intended to replace professional help. If you are out of control (or someone else is), or you're afraid someone will get hurt, find help immediately.

The words **Pause**, **Acknowledge**, **Reflect**, **Decide**, and **Act** will remind you to focus on the PARDA Process and work with the steps. You'll read examples from others' experiences and how to flow from one step to another. You have choices for choosing strategies.

People using the PARDA Process have told me if they make one slight consistent change in their lives, the results somehow spill over unnoticed. When they decide to make their bed each morning, they started hanging up their clothes, so they don't wrinkle the bedspread. When they're tired after arriving home from work, they put things away out of habit instead of dropping everything on the floor. Their goal to declutter the bedroom and create long-lasting habits of neatness grew without pushing.

Within the five steps of the PARDA Process are techniques and ideas to mix and match around your temperament. Be playful. Find what works for you and tailor your steps to your goals.

This is a process and is meant to be used in multiple ways that best suit your needs in the moment.

- When you finish a project, or come to a natural break, **Pause** and mentally skim through the steps multiple times each day to refresh and focus yourself.
- Resolve emotional upsets or confusion at the time they occur to identify what is going on inside before you lash out or do something you regret.
- Problem-solve. The PARDA Process steps will help you sort things out.

The more you use it, and take time to delve deeply, the better you will be able to solve problems and create sustained change.

But It's Too Simple

People tell me my suggestions are too simple or downright silly. I include them because:

- They allow for choice.
- They're easy.
- They're based on small steps to ease the terror of risk.
- They let us remain calm in the heat of the moment.
- They flex between thinking and action.
- They incorporate religious principles—or not.
- They're easy enough for children and tweens to understand and use.

During a crisis, skim the surface to get back in balance. Or, take time to dig deeper for understanding by writing about your experiences as you go through the process. Work at your own pace and decide how deep you want to explore. The more you invest a few minutes in any practice—the PARDA Process or any other skill—taking action becomes easier.

You might agonize, "Am I doing this right? What if it doesn't work?" Stop fretting and *always* treat yourself gently. The PARDA acronym will help you recall the steps in sequence when you're under pressure.

There's No Quick Fix

"That's not fair!" cry youngsters when a sibling gets more cookies or a bigger toy than a sister or brother. It's also what adults mutter when they're passed over for a coveted promotion. We know by the time we're young adults that life isn't fair. We see suffering, and we wonder why some people have it harder than they deserve. We shrink away from tragedy out of a primitive fear that it will contaminate us.

But there's no quick fix—never has been. Crash diets crash. It's easy to give up instead of plan to save money for a down payment for a house, let alone for retirement.

Cal Newport, professor and author of the book *Deep Work: Rules for Focused Success in a Distracted World*, has terrific tips on maintaining focus. His Study Hacks blog (http://calnewport.com) is loaded with suggestions for students on how to study and excel in college. Scrolling through the posts, however, you'll realize the content applies to everyone, not just students.

While looking at his blog postings, I found one from October 21, 2009 titled "The Hidden Art of Practice."[4] Newport described how skillful he's become at dealing with his email without wasting time. His next few sentences, however, caught my attention. He wrote: "It took years of practice to get to this efficient state." He went on to say, ". . . regardless of how simple my suggestion is, it's still going to take practice to make it a reliable part of your life."

I felt vindicated. Finally, someone told the truth and admitted *change takes time*.

Change Takes Effort

Change thrives on repetition and practice. After reading Cal Newport's blog post, I realized everyone struggles to change habits and/or learn new skills. I create and sustain change is by practicing an activity until it becomes a habit or become skillful enough to do it without straining. It takes time. It takes practice. Unfortunately, there isn't an easier way.

When you understand that change takes time and effort, you're primed to commit to whatever it takes to get a problem solved. The challenge is to make the effort without giving up in exhaustion or, worse, despair.

Darryl "DMC" McDaniels wrote in his book *Ten Ways Not to Commit Suicide,* he grew up in church hoping God would make things better. He finally realized he wouldn't get better until he sought counseling and worked on his own life. This is why "bottoming out" is a way many people reach the point of deciding to work at change. "What mattered was that I was trying to play an active role in my own salvation," he wrote.[5]

There has always been tension between "working out your salvation with fear and trembling" (Philippians 2:12) and walking by faith. Like Darryl McDaniels, you need to decide how much you want to commit to the work of healing and change.

This is where the PARDA Process shows a way to ease into making specific changes in your life.

Not only is there no quick fix but often change isn't enjoyable. We expect that arduous work should be fun. Consequently, we cheat ourselves of the satisfaction of a difficult job well done. Another benefit of sticking to things is knowing we can deal with tough times and come out the other end.

The resulting core of inner strength I didn't have earlier makes up for the struggle. I'll trade that for fun any time.

There is no quick fix; however, small actions have worked. To create a sustained change, I learned to build on small steps over time. The Japanese call this *kaizen*, the concept of continuous improvement. (Chapter 9 explores the concept of micromoves, which is my version of *kaizen*.)

A Process, Not a Cure

Don't despair if you find yourself struggling with the same issue again and again. Many Christians are floored when they slip into sin. They either give up on the Christian life or beat themselves up for being horrible sinners. Both extremes are wrong. That's why it's important to be kind to yourself.

The PARDA Process is an ongoing practice that allows for change and problem-solving over time. Yes, you will make mistakes. Yes, you will fail. And yes, you will pick yourself up and go back to the process.

The PARDA Process doesn't replace time alone with God when you ask Him to make the necessary changes in your heart. If you must choose between the PARDA Process or spending time with God, please select time with Him. It's tempting to read Christian books or do fellowship with other believers as replacements for spending time alone with God and His Word.

I've pondered what I should tell people who ask me for advice or help. What ideas could I pass on, especially if it seems they don't know how to think? They look online and talk to acquaintances, but they don't take time to figure out solutions for themselves. The word "think" gave me a clue.

The business world opened my eyes to strategic thinking, followed by planning and implementation. Organizations want defined outcomes and value the steps required to achieve them. Young solo entrepreneurs embrace failure as a learning process and have leapfrogged over big companies bringing successful products to market. They've learned how to think.

People fall into two mindsets, and I've been in both places at one time or another. The first is to be passive and believe God will fix all our problems with no effort on our part. The second is to charge ahead in a flurry of activity and collapse in exhaustion.

Then because there has been little or no improvement despite our efforts, we're bitter.

Too many of us lack a consistent way to think through problems and habits. If we get to the point of creating a plan, how do we implement the changes? I've experienced God's intervention in certain situations that had no human solution. But that's rare. Usually God hides His face and moves with glacial slowness. He didn't wave a celestial wand and fix all my personality quirks in an instant.

That's why I developed this process, one I stick in the hip pocket of my mind to apply as needed. It had to be flexible enough to use in a crisis when I didn't have time to think straight. Or, if I wanted to explore the issue further, it would give me a way to take it deeper.

Most techniques I'd learned over time felt lopsided. Some were great for exploring possibilities and correcting erroneous thinking. Others emphasized insight as a means of generating change. Most of them, however, lacked strategies for getting up and doing something.

This observation brought up questions:

- How do I corral all the techniques that seemed to work?
- How do I make sure they help someone else?
- How do I balance thinking, feeling, and action?
- How do I keep my actions simple and stop agonizing?
- Are they simple actions that become a regular part of my life?
- Are they biblical, and do they honor God?

Yes, it's easy to meditate and visualize, but do I follow through and act to bring the visualization to pass? It's a mistake to expect visualization as a magical fix while ignoring the effort involved to achieve goals or change habits.

More than that, what tactics will heal problems and situations in my life? If I can't change something, how do I live with it and remain detached? It's not my place to change others, although heaven knows, I've tried—with disastrous results.

"God grant me the serenity to accept the things I cannot change, the courage to change the things I can, and the wisdom to know the difference." – Reinhold Niebuhr

We all struggle with change and acceptance. Which is best? We need wisdom to know the difference, but if we weren't taught thinking skills, how do we think it through, let alone decide? (Chapter 7 explores the need for thinking and planning in an age when these skills seem to be lost.)

Long-range Goals and Personal Change

We have become a culture that thrives on speed. Commercials and articles tout the virtues of speed. We see drivers who weave in and out of traffic in their haste to get ahead, and we end up behind them at a stoplight watching them fume.

When did rushing, hurrying, and multitasking become admirable traits?

Many Japanese and Chinese firms have been around for hundreds of years. They don't have quarterly business plans unless you count those that mark 25 years—a quarter century. I recall sitting in a meeting years ago with several Asian businessmen who methodically planned the next 100-plus years of their company. They pored over demographic projections, societal trends, computer-generated data, and other factors to discern how to lead their company into the future.

Later in the day, I spoke with them as we sipped tea. Curious, I asked how they could plan so far ahead. "We plan for our companies to be here three and four hundred years from now. Things will change, yes. But we have a plan we can change as needed." They went on to say, "You Americans are too young. You have been here for less than three hundred years. You have no sense of the future."

Despite their propensity for long-term planning, Japanese business owners and managers implement change with simple steps, resulting in minute improvements that accumulate over time. "We have learned to think quickly. Ideas are welcome from both managers and factory workers," I was told. From them, I first learned the concept of *kaizen* or continuous improvement, which became the basis for the "micromoves" concept.

The conversation over tea stayed with me. I saw companies hire students with MBAs but minimal business experience to head up divisions. "We need fresh thoughts, new blood," the managers said. The young, inexperienced graduates were determined to initiate huge changes to improve corporate profits. They had no understanding of corporate culture and the value of employee experience.

I wonder how my life would have been different if I'd thought twenty, thirty, or fifty years into the future while in my teens? What if I had sat down for an hour or two in my early twenties and written down a brief description of what I wanted for my life? It's never too late to start.

Take Responsibility for Your Choices

Until you are comfortable with the PARDA Process, start by using it on situations *you* adjust and change. Then keep your lips zipped until your new habits are firmly in place.

On the other hand, some people find it helpful to announce to the world they're tackling a new diet or running a marathon. Public pressure helps rather than hinders them.

If you need to involve someone else in your decision to make changes such as reducing debt or exercising more, proceed with caution. There can be blowback to reducing the number of meals or bringing down debt if you don't include others.

One stay-at-home mom was livid at her husband's decision to cut back on their restaurant spending to reduce their debt. She snarled, "You get to go out to lunch with clients, but I have to suffer from your decision for both of us to eat in on the weekends.

I sure don't see you cooking a meal." Her husband's choice made things worse for her, despite his good intentions. He would have been wise to involve his wife in his plans.

Whenever you decide to make a change, ask yourself if this is your choice. When you're forced into change by someone else's ultimatum, you will fail. You cannot live for your parents, best friend, or spouse. Otherwise, resentment builds, or you act out by being passive-aggressive. Instead, make it *your* choice. Always understand you have choices, rather than being forced into a box.

"Part of getting a second chance is taking responsibility for what you did wrong in the first place." – Jack Bauer

By taking ownership of your PARDA Process and moving ahead at your own pace, you're sending a message to your brain, heart, and psyche. Small, repeated action steps prove you're serious about walking the talk.

Keep the Goal in Mind

By keeping written notes, you return to issues as needed or record more material. Your notes are a safe holding place when download the thoughts darting through your mind. Getting the thoughts out on paper frees up mental space and provides distance from the issues. The mind and body don't have to keep track of it all. It takes the pressure off.

Record your progress. My little notebook keeps me accountable by documenting how many tasks I complete over the weekend and what I need to do. When I record my successes, it's a personal pat on the back and justifies my rewards. It doesn't nag me to do more.

If something in your life has failed, write that down as well, painful as it feels. Think of it is as feedback and part of your process, not failure. When you make tiny changes on a problem, subsequent steps become easier. The situation seems solvable, and solutions you didn't know existed show up.

You find hope.

Get Started

When creating the PARDA Process, I sought to make it easy yet focused. Here are a few suggestions:

- If all you do is **Pause** for now, that's okay.
- Sequence is important. A few minutes spent on **Pause**, **Acknowledge,** and **Reflect** will reap dividends down the line when it comes to **Decide** and **Act**.
- Take your time with the various steps since some issues will take longer than others. Planning a job change or moving away takes more effort than getting in the habit of properly putting files away.
- Scribble a note when an insight strikes you or take a moment to record information about options to examine later. Think in minute details.
- Track which tools work best for you. Lists? If-then statements? Recording the date and time of projects? Experiment. Keep it light. You will gravitate toward some tools but not others.
- Be adventurous. Even if you don't think something will work, try it anyway.
- I can't say it enough: stop beating yourself up. Would you treat your best friend the way you treat yourself?
- Write down what works to ensure you'll remember it. Better to trust the palest ink over the strongest brain.

I keep telling people to write down their thoughts because this is where the greatest change takes place. There are several pages devoted to taking notes, and I repeat instructions often. This is deliberate. Chapter 6, Reflection, goes into greater detail about writing dumps and rants.

When you start something new, you'll find yourself spending more time than expected. Ease into the process by writing notes to yourself during the day—short phrases are fine. Stick the notes in your purse, your wallet, or the pockets of your jeans or jacket. At the end of the day, gather them, then scribble a few lines in a notebook or journal. *No one* should see these "scribbles." Then find a safe place to keep your notebook.

Writing notes by hand focuses your body and brain. Your notes will range from expressing unpleasant thoughts to insights you've received throughout the day. Be sure to write down the pleasant events that struck your fancy, such as the compliment you received or the soft colors of sunset. Record these thoughts to capture them before they slip away. Go back and look at them to remind yourself of pleasant experiences.

More suggestions:

- Take time to look at your notes. This will help you track changes and recall ideas or thoughts about a situation or challenge. Go deep; more ideas will pop up when you honor your writing and thinking processes.
- Find a specific time to create the habit of automatically writing a few sentences. It isn't necessary to do this daily in the beginning, since people who have never kept a journal find it too difficult. I already have a writing process in the morning, so as the day goes on, I use the PARDA Process in my head while in the thick of things. This keeps me grounded when my emotions run high or I feel cranky. I scribble notes to myself, and then transcribe them into my journal.
- Be easy on yourself. While it's great to write daily, you're better off writing for five or ten minutes every few days initially. Forcing yourself makes it too easy to give up. The goal? To create a consistent habit and make the process as effortless as possible.

When you become familiar with the PARDA Process, you will **Pause** before you act. You'll think through a situation instead of beating yourself up for mistakes. While the second half of this book has several situations as examples for using the PARDA Process, I know you'll find many more.

The more you create the habit of using the PARDA Process, the more comfortable you become and the easier it will feel.

"Habit is habit, and not to be flung out of the window by any man, but coaxed downstairs one step at a time." – Mark Twain

Chapter 2

Pause

Get on with it," I hear you saying. "How does this work?"

The individual steps are simple and roll seamlessly into each other as you work through the process. Take time, start small. Experiment.

If you find you're scared of the emotions that arise, please seek professional help.

Pause, Not Stop

People have asked me why I say **Pause** instead of Stop. To me, Stop feels abrupt. There's an intimidating quality to Stop. It's urgent. Right now.

Pause feels better. It's softer, yielding. Pausing allows me to slow down, rather than come to a screeching halt like a car at an unexpected stop sign. When I **Pause**, it's for enjoyable experiences, not just when I'm too exhausted to continue.

Try it right now. Stop reading, take a soft breath or three or four of them. **Pause** lets you orient yourself to the here and now. Let your muscles loosen. Your brain slows down, but don't force it to go blank. Avoid hyperventilating.

What you're trying to do here is called diaphragmatic breathing. The goal is to breathe deeply and gently from your belly, instead of shallow breaths from your chest, which will automatically raise your heart rate and cause anxiety. Watch a little baby. When she is on her back, you can clearly see her tummy rising and falling—not her chest.

Start by counting to four on the inhale and taking eight counts for the exhale. Your belly should be expanding on the inhale and contracting effortlessly on the exhale. For many of us, we do exactly the opposite. The chest expands and contracts. Or, our belly contracts as we inhale, and the breath remains in the chest.

One way to practice is lie on your back on the floor. Place a lightweight book on your stomach, and watch it rise and fall while you breathe. Observe air going in and out without making any changes for a minute or two. While I learned this from my mother when I was a child, I still check myself often to make sure I'm breathing from my stomach, and not my chest.

Did you bother to **Pause**, or did you keep reading without missing a beat? That's okay, just keep reading and try again later.

I **Pause** because I tend to feel anxious for no particular reason and have learned it's because I've shifted into taking fast, shallow breaths from my chest. Furthermore, I have a habit of shooting from the lip before my brain is engaged. I tell myself to put a sock in it before it gets worse. Yes, I still blurt things out, but I've (hopefully) improved based on the fewer number of apologies I've had to give during the past several years.

If you're having a problem learning diaphragmatic breathing, find a sports trainer or exercise instructor to get you started. Use this form of breathing multiple times during the day when you **Pause** for your practice sessions. It will get easier, I promise.

When you **Pause**, especially when you're angry or upset, those precious few seconds keep you from making mistakes you regret later. Children, for example, push parents' buttons harder than anything I know. If parents and caregivers paused more, fewer children might be struck or scolded. Pesky drivers? Road rage is an all-too-common situation in many cities. If drivers would **Pause**, lives could be saved.

I don't know if this is a woman thing or what, but **Pause** is hard for me. I can't sit for long until I get up and put the clean dishes away or straighten the bedroom. What would happen if I slowed down? Why does the thought of **Pause** terrify me? What am I running away from?

The Benefits of Pause

When you **Pause** and breathe, take a moment to roll your shoulders or shake your hips. Many people (including me) carry tension in their necks and shoulders. Where is there tension in your body when **Pause**? Breathe into a tight place or into a ball of tension between your shoulders. **Pause** and be with the sensation without analyzing it. When thoughts arise, let them go. More thoughts will come in, and you will examine them later. For now, remain in stillness.

While **Pause** is good for you alone, it works wonders in relationships. When your kids sass you back or your spouse comes home crabby, try pausing and taking a breath to defuse situations before they escalate.

Pausing makes room for listening. When you don't rush to give an answer, people sense they're being heard and talk more openly. Taking time lets people respond at their pace. Wait. Value what they say by listening without interruption. Listening is tiring. It's hard work. The payoff is huge.

Pause frequently during the day with two or three slow breaths. Start by doing this when you first sit down at your desk and again at lunch time. Use cues such as a ringing phone to remind yourself to breathe throughout the day. Practice diaphragmatic breathing by identifying cues and making **Pause** a habit.

"Sometimes you need to hit pause to let everything sink in" – Sebastian Vettel

Before moving on to something else, stop. Breathe. Take a few sips of water. In fact, for all the steps, give yourself a few minutes to breathe and hydrate. I used to roll my eyes when people told me I needed to stay hydrated but drinking water throughout the day improved my thinking and decreased fatigue.

I found myself slowing down and becoming more focused when I paused. This in and of itself reduced my impulsive words. It reduced spending money and saying "yes" to commitments I later regretted. The more complex issues became grist for my journal.

Along with gentle breathing, take a few moments to use all your senses. **Pause** and take a sniff. What do you smell? When I was kid, I used to sniff various rooms in our house. From that, I knew when my folks had relatives over after I'd gone to bed. One aunt smelled like Chanel No. 5 perfume and cigarettes. My uncle who worked as a carpenter smelled of sweat, wood, and a different brand of tobacco. My dad? No. 2 diesel fuel from being on the tugboat all day. It drove my parents nuts trying to figure out how I knew who had stopped by. They didn't believe I could smell people.

I sniff around when I enter a store or restaurant. What are they cooking? Is there a strong odor of stale grease, or is my mouth watering in anticipation of tasty food? When we've been away from home for several days and our house has been closed, when I open the door it smells like a used bookstore. The air is stale, but I never tire of the odor of books.

What colors do you see? How many variations of yellow or blue do you see when you look at a clump of flowers? Sounds? Explore your sense of touch by running your fingers along a wooden staircase, or the push of your muscles when you get out of a chair. Take a look at Appendix C, 101+ Ways to Pause and Savor for additional sensory examples to use when you **Pause**.

Cultivating **Pause** in my life taught me the joy of savoring. I learned to enjoy what I touched, smelled, tasted. Gradually I've become enamored of stillness, of sensing the world slowing down and its beauty increasing.

When to Pause

Use **Pause** to set priorities. Resist being sucked into thinking that all the demands placed upon you and your time are equally important. When asked to take on another responsibility, **Pause** and think about the ramifications on your time and energy. You know the drama queens and kings who have an uncanny ability to suck you into their upsets. A **Pause** will let you *act* instead of *reacting* to their demands.

Better still, take extended periods of **Pause**. A friend of mine said her husband came home after a stressful day and got into their whirlpool. For her, the novelty of doing this wore off, but for her husband, it became a way to unwind for an hour or more.

Do you **Pause** for a day? A weekend? Do you take extended time to slow down, to be in the moment by exploring how your body feels? What do you see? What do you sense around you? Is where you are right now warm and stuffy, or do you feel cool breezes?

A challenge is taking the kind of downtime you enjoy rather than going to the newest trendy resort. What suits your temperament—being out in the woods or by the ocean? Walking in a city you've never seen before? What do you and your family find refreshing, and how can everyone's preferences be honored? Many people return to work to recuperate from their "vacation."

Build in regular **Pauses** to clarify your thinking, calm your racing body, and decide what is most important to you.

Why Are We So Scared to Pause?

It turns out I'm not the only one who's scared to stop and do nothing. Timothy Wilson, a social psychologist at the University of Virginia, wanted to see if people could sit quietly with themselves for at least fifteen minutes.[6] The rooms where he had them sit were sparsely furnished. Participants were instructed to put away their belongings, including cell phones and other objects. They were then asked to be alone with their thoughts.

Another group did the same thing, but it took place in their homes instead of a bland room. You would think this would be less of a problem, right? Wrong. It didn't matter how old the participants were, their environment, or their dependence on social media. Nobody really enjoyed their "time out," although they volunteered to participate in the experiment.

To complicate matters, at the beginning of the experiment, all participants were given an electric shock. It was uncomfortable enough that they were willing to pay the researcher not to receive another one. But when they learned they, too, could give themselves the same shock, more than 50% of the participants chose to self-administer another one when they were alone. In other words, *giving themselves a shock was less painful than being alone and undistracted with their thoughts.*

Humans are designed for activity. When we're busy, we're productive and others praise us for our busyness. We're stigmatized when we're idle. We assume we must always keep busy and enjoy the rush of crossing one more thing off our to-do list. I've experienced that surge of satisfaction, although much of what I did at the time was mundane such as running errands or doing laundry.

But do we have to be busy? Do we allow ourselves a conscious choice of what's important or what isn't? Much of what we do appears urgent but isn't important.

We have so much information coming at us from a multitude of sources that our brains can't discern the difference between importance and urgency. We're "running hot" 24/7. And the longer we do this, the harder it is to slow ourselves down, let alone disengage to pay attention to what we're thinking and sensing.

"He who can no longer pause to wonder and stand rapt in awe, is as good as dead; his eyes are closed." – Albert Einstein

No wonder we feel uncomfortable letting ourselves **Pause** for short periods, let alone taking it easy on a weekend or on vacation.

I've gotten better at **Pause** because my body rebelled at one point and I got sick. I had to pause whether I wanted to or not. In hindsight, there was so much happening at the same time. I was terrified that if I stopped, I'd curl up in a ball, fall apart and then nothing would get done. I was taking care of my mom, selling her home, and dealing with my own struggles. Looking back, I don't know how I did it all. God is my rock and my salvation, but my husband was my Rock of Gibraltar during those tough times.

Are we afraid to face ourselves? Most of us have ongoing, low levels of anxiety regarding unfinished business and unpleasant experiences we're scared to examine. That's why I suggest applying the PARDA Process to unwind and be comfortable in our own skin.

Chapter 3

Acknowledge

Acknowledgment demands honesty. When I ask you to **Acknowledge**, do so without condemnation or judgment as in "How could I have *said* that? Why did I forget?" If you're in a safe place, let 'er rip. Telling off your boss at work or the police officer who pulled you over isn't smart.

When you **Acknowledge** an event, describe it as though you're explaining it to someone from another planet. "I was supposed to get the sales report to the vice president on Monday, and the figures were wrong." Notice what you are physically experiencing as well as the internal feelings and voices in your head as you say this. This is hard. You find yourself thinking, "Oh, that's terrible. I shouldn't think that." Or, "Boy, was I ever stupid. How could I do such a thing?" Stop the snotty comments to yourself and remain detached. State thoughts and emotions without self-condemnation.

Stop shooting yourself in the foot with sarcastic mental put-downs. "This will never work." "These small moves won't amount to much." "I've tried to (lose weight, get organized, etc.) before and it hasn't worked." Sound familiar? You beat yourself up more than anyone else would, including friends and loved ones. Why?

I spend lots of time telling people how to **Acknowledge** to avoid getting trapped in emotional loops. Until you reach the point when you **Acknowledge** what you're feeling in the moment without judging and beating yourself up, your emotions will keep you trapped.

Let yourself be curious. Trust that any unpleasant emotions and discomfort will shift and pass. You're safe. What if you feel uncomfortable with "bad" feelings such as shame, guilt, and anger? What if I told you they have a role in your life? Those "good" feelings sure feel wonderful, but they keep you stuck in your comfort zone. All emotions serve a purpose.

Don't analyze what happened, at least not now. You'll see how the chapter on **Reflect** explores this more deeply.

The Challenge of Exploring Feelings and Emotions

There have been long-running discussions on how to define the words "emotions" and "feelings." For simplicity's sake, I use both words interchangeably.

Trying to **Acknowledge** by separating emotions and events is hard. We don't want to experience unpleasant thoughts and emotions. We're afraid they will overwhelm us, and we'll shatter. We find it difficult to separate emotions from self-condemnation. To complicate matters further, our bodies flood us with chemicals that make it difficult to remain calm and think clearly. Our breathing becomes fast and shallow, making us anxious.

Most of us grew up in homes where expressing feelings appropriately wasn't modeled by our parents, relatives, and friends. Many of us have memories of unpleasant fights or periods of steaming silence. My folks loved each other deeply. I seldom saw them disagree, but they were uncomfortable with tears, outbursts, and the like. They both had a stiff upper lip that made Englishmen look like wimps.

What were your meals like growing up? Did everyone talk until you felt unheard? Or did you sit politely and limit conversation to superficialities? Were there arguments? Were you able to talk to one or both parents before bed about your day?

Think about the sheer range of emotions that exist: anger, joy, sadness, excitement, and more. Less clearly defined feelings such as boredom or restlessness are hard to articulate. Emotions fluctuate in intensity depending on our temperament and age. No wonder we struggle to use them appropriately.

We believe anger is wrong, that always feeling happy should be our default mode. We stifle feelings we think are inappropriate, but our bodies respond with headaches, tight shoulders, and the like. We deny our emotions at our peril.

Yet emotions explored with compassion have their place and add richness to our lives. Most of us use either emotion or logic to solve our problems, but neither one is better than the other. One of the goals for the PARDA Process is to flex back and forth between emotions and thinking. It aims to honor all aspects of our personality rather than pick one because we wrongly think it's better than another.

Does this mean I believe in always "telling it like it is" regardless of the situation or consequences? No way. Learning appropriate expression of our emotions is a huge part of maturity. We all know adults who act like children and youngsters who show self-control beyond their years.

Allow Painful Emotions to Emerge

When you take time to **Acknowledge**, explore what your body is feeling. When I'm feeling ashamed for being late even though it was because of a train delay, I experience a flushing sensation in my face. My muscles get tense and my breathing quickens. I realize I let someone down.

Being in a state of acknowledgment requires compassionately allowing painful emotions to emerge rather than pushing them away. You know you're succeeding when you feel your body relax and unclench. Your jaw muscles loosen your fingers uncurl. Little by little, the intensity subsides, and you move away from feeling upset. When you first explore your feelings, they clamor for attention and you wonder if you'll get through them all. Again, and again, I encourage people to be kind to themselves, to console their inner toddler whose emotions are running rampant. You can't get through to a child in the middle of a tantrum or reach your girlfriend who's having a meltdown over something at work. By acknowledging the anguish despite your "logical" brain telling you "it's no big deal," you're honoring *all* of you, not just the "nice" parts of your personality.

Those "bad" emotions of fear, doubt, shame, and guilt act as reminders. Fear reminds us to be careful in potentially dangerous situations. Doubt allows us to check our actions before we do something stupid. Shame and guilt remind us of our connection to humanity, so we try to avoid causing harm to ourselves and others.

I'm Smiling If It Kills Me

Norman Vincent Peale was the grandfather of positive thinking. His books were filled with stories of people who thought positively and experienced improvements in their lives. Many of them have a Horatio Alger, rags-to-riches feel. You wonder, "Why do I think positively, yet everything in my life goes from bad to worse?"

Here's why. Forcing yourself to deny your sadness, anger, or grief leaves them stuck inside your body and mind with no place to go. Rather than denying your emotions, **Acknowledge** what you're feeling in the moment—without judgment. Unfortunately, service providers such as baristas and sales clerks are not allowed the luxury in the moment of acknowledging their feelings despite interactions with angry customers. They are forced to offer fake smiles, and the physical and emotional toll is draining.[7]

Try this experiment. The next time you realize you're beating yourself up over something bad or stupid, **Pause** and gently breathe three or four times. Let the heated emotion subside and tell yourself in the third person, "Gee, interesting. 'Julie, do you wonder why you did...?'" or, "Poor Julie, that situation pushed her buttons. Could it be she's overtired and needs a break?"

Continue to be tentative and curious. In these moments, be kind to yourself. Talk to yourself in the third person like a loving friend. Don't wait to craft the perfect statement. Instead, jump in and start talking to yourself.

Do You Want Cheese and Crackers with That Whine?

We feel sorry for ourselves and think no one has it as bad as we do. Are there times we need to think about how other people struggle with bratty kids? Deal with unemployment? Experience depression and struggle? Instead, we get on our pity pot and feel sorry for ourselves.

Again, don't beat yourself up, but do realize others have been in the same situation. **Acknowledge** the anger, self-pity, or embarrassment and let it go. This is where you're at in this moment, and if you stop stuffing them down, your emotions will shift.

I've gotten to the point (most of the time) of reminding myself repeatedly, "You've had problems before and you will get through them yet again." I talk to myself like a small child and say, "You're scared. You're panicked." I remind myself this happened before, and it will happen again. Then I say, "You survived and will survive again." In this way, I let myself feel the fear of certain situations. This is helpful when I awaken in the middle of the night, fretting over events from earlier in the day.

Pay Attention and Describe the Emotion and Experience

A huge part of **Acknowledge** in the PARDA Process is paying attention to what we're feeling. We deny the intensity of our grief and remain stuck, unable to move on. Anger tells us when our boundaries are violated. Our earliest ancestors relied on fear to outwit large animals that saw them as a tasty snack. We need our emotions, and we ignore them at our peril. This means allowing us to **Acknowledge** our unpleasant emotions instead of stuffing them down.

While you are within a situation, **Acknowledge** what's occurring. Describe your feelings and thoughts in the moment. If this includes four-letter words, let them out. "My heart is racing. I want to punch my coworker in the nose. How could he be such a jerk?" Allow the waves of emotion to pass through your body while you breathe slowly.

When you hear words and phrases going through your mind, verbalize them. Better still, write them down, no matter how small or trivial. What is your internal tape saying? Is it relevant to what's happening in the present? Or is it old "stuff" from years ago, from people who have died or are no longer part of your life, such as a grammar school teacher? Deepen the situation and purge it from your system by doing a writing dump.

Tell Your Story as an Observer

Step back and recall painful memories. When we recall them, we re-experience the events in our bodies as if we're immersed in the event right now. Our blood pressure rises, we curl into ourselves, and take shallow breaths.

Instead of closing into yourself, pretend you're watching events unfold as if you're watching a DVD or YouTube. Observe yourself in the situation and notice what's going on around you. Who else is there? What do you see around the participants? How did this event occur? Studies reveal cognitive shifts and detachment occur when volunteers distance themselves from painful experiences as they recall them. They keep the memories, but the emotional charge dissipates, and insights arise while exploring the experience.

From this detached point of view, isolate a painful event and describe the scene in the third person. Take a moment to speculate what else was going on or why the event occurred.

Here's a story I wrote in third person about an event in my life. "Nancy's supervisor told the students they didn't need to follow through on her requests. According to her, Nancy was being far too strict. The students didn't need to turn in their assignments on time."

While writing these words, I recall the shelving in the supervisor's office as she spoke. I see stacks of papers about to topple over on her desk. Some students look confused, while others are smiling, happy they don't have to do the assignments. I wrote how hurt I felt, not to mention angry and undermined.

When I wrote about this in the third person years later, I began to question the underlying motives. What was the reason for the encounter? Was I indeed being too strict? Might the supervisor have resented me for working with the students when she could no longer do so? The woman was close to retirement, while I was younger. Did I pose a threat? Who knows or cares? The memory bothered me for years trying to figure out what happened.

Once I began describing this event and my emotions in the third person, everything settled. After that, it became a memory I seldom thought about. When I ran into my old supervisor years later, I knew the emotional charge was gone. She had retired less than six months after I left. When we met, I could greet her with a smile and polite indifference. I noticed the deep grooves at the edges of her mouth. She looked thinner and had aged. She nodded and walked away.

Brent's Story

When you write, be precise in your description by engaging all your senses. A client named Brent told me about an incident that happened years ago—one that bugged him today. He said, "Jason, my project leader at the time, wanted a presentation on how the department was going to handle cost overruns on a redesign of a client's computer system. I spent hours with another engineer crunching the numbers. It turned out the client kept making changes to the original design or wanted additional programs at no cost.

"Before the presentation, our graphics admin did a PowerPoint with some jazzy illustrations. Dave from Accounting did the numbers for the charts. I looked it over, sure, but I'm the design person, not the numbers guy. We all thought it was good to go, including Jason."

Brent swallowed and stared at the floor. He described the beige walls, the whiteboard with calculations written in red and black, the meeting room with no windows, which smelled of recycled air.

"I started explaining the charts and began to realize the numbers didn't add up the way I thought they did. Other people in the meeting pointed out the mistakes. Jason told me I had let the entire department down, that I'd done a terrible job as presenter.

"I kept going back over the presentation, looking for what I could have done differently, but I couldn't figure it out. Luckily, I got a job offer from a buddy in another company, so I left. It wasn't exactly what I wanted, but I knew my days at this job were numbered—Jason would make sure of that."

Eight years later, Brent still felt he had messed up, although as he told the story, it seemed to me he was Jason's scapegoat. To this day, he checks and rechecks his work, terrified of another humiliating mistake. Recounting the story to me, he thought about a meeting with an engineer and someone from Accounting prior to the presentation.

"Yeah, now that I think about it, there was no way Jason would have turned us loose in the first place unless he had checked the figures himself several times. He had meetings with Dave and me plus people in the engineering department."

I could see Brent's eyes become unfocused. His breathing slowed. He began to see what I had already suspected. Jason would not have allowed the meeting to occur if anything was wrong with the figures. Jason and David were responsible for the errors they had let slip, not Brent.

"It wasn't just me. Jason, the jerk, used me. I wasn't totally to blame after all! And then I left the company because of him." Brent was processing his realization.

Reflecting on this painful event paid off by helping Brent understand there was more to the story. The shame and humiliation he felt blinded him to what had happened. Thanks to this experience, Brent realized he had become more careful and conscientious in subsequent projects, which led him to being in line for a promotion if he wanted it.

"I didn't realize how much I had stopped trying for promotions out of fear I would make another mistake," Brent told me. We met again once or twice, and the last I heard, he had moved up to district manager.

Acknowledging his shame and embarrassment was crucial to Brent's understanding about what had happened. Once his emotions cooled, he could reflect on the experience and decide what to do next. He had no guarantees, of course, that he wouldn't make mistakes in the future, but the experience made him a better team leader.

What is your story? Write about the event and **Acknowledge** your feelings. Scribbling it out lets you detach and remove the material from your head without losing the details or becoming trapped by feelings.

The Feeling Beneath the Experience

When I think about an unpleasant experience, emotions wash through me. Shame. Guilt. Embarrassment. Anger. Combinations of the above.

Contrast this with memories of fun with friends. I suggest when you recall a pleasant experience, immerse yourself in the happiness and laughter you felt, and let that flow through your body.

When you **Acknowledge** and write down your experiences, always include what you're feeling, no matter how raw. Let emotions flow without self-condemnation. When upsetting emotions are triggered, grab your notebook and find a private spot. If you're at the office and have an open cubicle, head for a bathroom stall for privacy. You have the best of intentions to write when you get home, but that seldom happens. Instead, you'll be tempted to stuff down the tears and emotions as if nothing had happened. Several hours later, the intensity will be gone, and you'll minimize how upset you felt in that moment.

When you write, track those feelings. If you can't describe the emotion, describe the sensation and location in your body. "My chest is tight. My neck muscles are tight. It's hard to catch my breath." Name the emotion in a general way, and let clarity arise later.

Don't worry about being totally accurate. If your sense is "I'm so (expletive) mad I could scream," write it down and **Acknowledge** it. People tell me, "But I'm not sure I know what I'm feeling." That's fine. **Pause**. Take a few breaths. If nothing comes up, go with the tiniest bit you have. "I'm scared" may be all you can face right now. It's okay. Let it go.

You may realize what else you're feeling after you get home or when you wake up in the morning. Once I became used to sitting in my discomfort, I could calm down and feel less fearful. I figured out that just because I had an unpleasant experience, I didn't have to be afraid it would take over. Curiosity let me hold unpleasant sensations long enough to examine what happened. When my emotions subsided, I could think again.

Avoid beating yourself up about your feelings. We'll go into greater depth about your feelings in **Reflect**.

When You Can't Write

If the situation is too painful and you can't write, **Pause**, breathe, and breathe again. Experiment by describing the event in the third person out loud while retaining as much exactitude and focus as possible.

The more I've honored what I'm thinking and feeling, especially by writing it down, the faster my vulnerable places uncurled. It took a while, but scribbling words and fragments seemed to convey to my innermost self I was serious about acknowledging parts of me I'd ignored or, worse, denied and pushed down.

While emotions feel intense at times, the more you **Acknowledge** your feelings, the faster the intensity subsides. Then it's easier to think clearly. Scientists have found that animals who escape their enemies or experience a fright continue to stand and tremble after reaching a safe place. In a moment or two, they start munching grass. That tells us animals do not live for hours in hyper-alert mode, and neither should humans. It is far easier to live in the moment than hold on to emotions. Doctors, scientists, and other professionals have documented the harmful effects of ongoing stress, anxiety, and fear. Nevertheless, a frontal cortex, amygdala, reptilian brain, and other structures coexisting in one skull makes it harder to process and release unpleasant experiences.

Our Vulnerable Little Child

When you continue to make a practice of acknowledging what you're feeling in the moment, don't be surprised if earlier unpleasant memories pop up. As an adult, I realize much of my anxiety stems from being a kid who didn't hear what people said. Because of my hearing impairment, people thought I was rude and snobbish when I walked past them without responding to their greetings. I didn't realize what an impact these experiences had on me until much later. It has been a challenge to grieve those memories as they resurface. My journal serves as a holding place for memories and emotions tied to what I experienced in childhood but were too painful to examine until I was ready as an adult.

"Vulnerability is basically uncertainty, risk, and emotional exposure." – Brené Brown

All of us have a vulnerable part inside of us. Call it the child, the unconscious, the wounded soul, whatever. It's the part of us that needs comfort and safety. I suggest you treat your scared, fearful parts with kindness. Yes, it will take time for your inner child and vulnerable spirit to realize you won't stomp all over your frightened little self.

My hat is off to Brené Brown, Ph.D., who has done extensive research on vulnerability and shame. Her books *Daring Greatly* and *Rising Strong* are paeans to embracing who and what you are and letting the world know it. I'm working on being vulnerable, and I look to Dr. Brown for inspiration.

If your thoughts and emotions are too overwhelming—if you're endlessly recalling a trauma or images from rape or war linger in your mind—then get up, walk around, get a drink of water, and let your pounding heart subside. Don't be heroic and try to resolve a high level of trauma by yourself. Get professional for your pain. Turn to the PARDA Process for the everyday upsets, habits, and issues that happen to all of us.

Acknowledge Now, Act Later

When you **Acknowledge** what's happening by using the PARDA Process, you realize you don't have to act on your thoughts in the moment. You think, "I love my kid, but I've had it with her back talk. My head hurts. I know I'm not supposed to, but I'd like to smack her one."

When you **Acknowledge,** it's tempting to feel ashamed of what you're expressing, and cut it off. But arguing with your internal dialogue or suppressing those tight feelings in the moment makes things worse. If the situation continues to escalate, again, walk away. Get a drink of water. Breathe slowly. Simmer down.

Years ago, a therapist said to me, "Just sit in it. Don't argue, just acknowledge and observe." "Oh, I'm sweating" or, "I'm having trouble taking a deep breath." The recurring challenge is to stay with the thought in the moment when it feels awful emotionally and physically. Our bodies are not designed to remain at acute levels of anger or anxiety. Staying in the moment—that is, letting it pass through until you feel calm or drained—will defuse unpleasant physiological sensations sooner. When you start judging yourself, think of Henry James who wrote: "Be kind. Be kind. Be kind."

Make time to explore what happened. Journal or use a writing dump. Whose voice do you hear talking in your mind when things go wrong? A parent? A teacher? Be curious by asking, "I wonder what set me off? Is there an image? Is there another voice that is calm, realistic?" Explore without pushing. When you don't have answers immediately, hours later or the next morning a flash of memory or a random thought will occur.

I have this yappy internal voice that talks in a fast, high-pitched voice. "Oh my gosh, what's going to happen? You blew it now. How could you do such a thing?" "Ooh, you've got to get all this done NOW. You're rotten spoiled and stupid." (I haven't yet figured out whose voice that tone belongs to.)

"Healing doesn't mean the damage never existed. It means the damage no longer controls our life." - Akshay Dubey

Relish the Good Stuff

Especially practice the PARDA Process when things are going right. When was the last time you wallowed in an accomplishment? Heck, why not praise yourself? This is the time for you to brag on yourself inside. It's too easy to focus on what's going *wrong* instead of what's going *right* in your life.

This isn't to whitewash painful experiences but rather to discover opportunities to figure out what's going right and create more of the same. Do we fear that, if we're easy on ourselves or our kids, we'll go down the tubes and become lazy, ungrateful slobs? But if we loosen the reins on ourselves, imagine what good will happen.

Child psychologists and other professionals remind parents, teachers, and caregivers of small children to catch them "doing well" and praise them. Let's do that for ourselves. Praise yourself for a trivial task. Say to yourself, "Hey, you got the papers filed and the laundry done. Good job." It may feel silly, but so what? We praise others for their victories, so why not do the same for ourselves? I suspect that if we refill our tanks with self-praise, we're less tempted to reward ourselves with retail therapy. Perhaps we'll ease up and stop scolding ourselves altogether.

Write down what went right and refer to it regularly. You will roll your eyes in the future at trivial victories, but at the time, they were important to you. Rereading what you've written reminds you of those feel-good experiences and shows you how far you've come.

Do you ever wear a piece of jewelry that brings back good memories of being with a loved one? Or keep your child's clay pot on your desk to make you smile whenever you look at it? These items help us enjoy experiences again for a moment or two. Treat yourself to that enjoyment.

Try an experiment. Instead of figuring out what you're grateful about, capture tiny moments that gave you pleasure, such as kind words from a friend. A presentation that went well. The meal with a sibling. Tracking these tiny events without forcing yourself to feel grateful makes you aware of what's going right in your life. Go further and examine these notes. Figure out any patterns and add more enjoyable moments to your life.

Am I Doing This Right?

People ask me, "How do I know when I'm doing the steps of the PARDA Process right?"

Seriously, there's no way to screw up if you're being kind to yourself and acknowledging your feelings with compassion and without judgment. Expect failures. Stop looking for the perfect solution. Allow for mistakes. Be kind to yourself and your loved ones by taking the pressure off. This is why it's called the PARDA *Process*. The goal is ongoing growth and change, not perfection.

Whenever you set goals, it's easy go into all-or-nothing thinking. You were "good" for a week by eating properly, but on Saturday night you pigged out. You chowed down on pepperoni pizza and garlic bread. You had planned to eat one or two slices of pizza, but you kept eating. Before you knew it, you told yourself, "I've blown it, so I'll just finish it off."

The following day, your stomach's bloated and your jeans feel tight, but that's nothing compared to what's going on in your mind. "Man, I messed up big-time. I'm such a porker. I can't stop at one bite." Never mind the good habits you had for an entire week. You didn't allow for the fact you worked six hours of overtime earlier and was ready to party as a reward. And you love Mandy's pizza. You've just set yourself up for failure.

Professionals working in the addictions field discovered that, like dieting, staying clean or sober included multiple slips before addicts could remain sober for a year or longer. Failure is an inevitable part of the process. That's why it's critical to be kind to yourself. Don't beat yourself up for not getting a "A" as a grade when "B" is acceptable.

Now that I'm older, I'm not sure which is worse: driving myself and others with too-high standards or failing spectacularly in front of everyone. I'm terrified that if I don't strive to be one hundred percent perfect, I'll let everything go and nothing will get done, let alone done right. But when I stop pushing and striving, a funny thing happens. The work flows. Doing a tiny bit, day by day, gets the job done. Gradually, I feel less frazzled.

Are Emotions Wrong?

People have asked me if I'm against emotions. Good heavens, no. I enjoy the melting feeling in my heart when I hold a newborn baby or rub a puppy. Movies and books can make me cry. Having a range of emotions has enriched my life immeasurably. My concern arises when emotions cloud our thinking and lead to unwise choices.

Did you know that emotions are a product of the limbic system of the brain? Chemicals called neurotransmitters are produced in response to what we're experiencing. Another chemical, serotonin, is generated when we're in love or eating chocolate. No wonder we feel happy.

Advertisers manipulate our emotions to promote a brand by making us think we must have their products. We can't name the exact feeling, but desires for luxury cars and expensive jewelry are triggered by skillful ad campaigns.

Scientists used to believe the mind and body were separate entities. They called it dualism, which means reasoning took place in the brain while the body was the repository of emotion and instinct. Intense emotions such as joy or fear arose without conscious input from the mind.

However, new research narrows the gap between the mind and body. According to scientist Antonio Damasio, we make decisions by weighing multiple options and deciding which is best for us.[8] To his surprise, he found that emotions—not rational thinking alone—help us make decisions. His work with brain-injured patients showed that loss of emotions impaired their ability to make good decisions. He describes the case of Elliott, a businessman whose life fell apart after the removal of a brain tumor. Damasio saw no evidence of sadness, impatience, or other feelings. Furthermore, combined with the lack of emotion, it was a struggle for Elliott to make decisions. Rational thinking and reasoning are intertwined with feelings, and not separate, was his conclusion.

"When dealing with people, remember you are not dealing with creatures of logic, but creatures of emotion." - Dale Carnegie

Ancient cultures mention the heart (or kidneys) as the source of our emotions. Our language points to our bodies as sources of information we can't rationally explain. We say, "Something doesn't smell right," or "Something in my gut tells me..." We can't ignore our feelings or push them away. When we tell ourselves, "It wasn't that bad," or "I shouldn't be upset," we're minimizing what we feel. Worse, we're lying to ourselves. Then we wonder if we dare trust our own intuition and feelings.

On the other hand, we know people who call everything disastrous—from a hangnail to burnt potatoes. When we hear a girlfriend moaning about her latest romantic break-up, after the fourth or fifth time, we roll our eyes.

Our brains find it hard to set gradations, or levels, of feelings. In one sense, it can't. When our ancestors felt a jolt of fear at a sound in the bushes, it required racing away from the saber-tooth tiger to avoid winding up as cat food. The modern version is driving on the highway and having to make a quick decision about the car swerving ahead. Worry today could be the fear of losing our jobs, which means financial struggle.

How do we stop living in ongoing fear or anxiety? We start with **Acknowledge**.

Chapter 4

Acknowledging Painful Experiences

Like everyone else, I dislike anger, shame, guilt, and sadness. I'd much rather be upbeat all the time. I'm grateful today's psychologists and mental health professionals now focus on the positive instead of always searching for what's wrong.

Still, when you think about it, humans have been around for thousands of years. Unpleasant emotions serve a purpose, or we wouldn't have them. Our emotions ebb and flow, yet we insist on always being "up" because we believe dark emotions to be wrong or scary.

"It would be impossible to estimate how much time and energy we invest in trying to fix, change and deny our emotions—especially the ones that shake us at our very core, like hurt, jealousy, loneliness, shame, rage and grief." – Debbie Ford

A toddler will be screaming in frustration at his parents and ten minutes later be all smiles and hugs. Unlike adults, children are blessed with the ability to let their emotions flow. We need to learn from them. Think back to the animals who experience fright then let it go.

When we acknowledge the feelings and thoughts we deem unpleasant and write them out, they begin to lose their power over us. We make the time to search out their hidden meaning. It's like the saying "We're not angry for the reason we think."

Emotions are Fleeting

Have you ever watched clouds move across the sky? If the weather is threatening, the wind blows heavy gray billows ahead of the storm. On a calm June day, they look like cotton balls dotting a blue sky. Clouds are never stable, always changing. So are our emotions.

When I was a university instructor, we had to drop a student from our graduate program. I had to break the unwelcome news to Elaine, since I was the newest faculty member. When I told her she was dropped, she exploded. She screamed. She cried. At one point, she grabbed a heavy glass ashtray and threw it at me. Luckily, I ducked, and she missed. "My life is over! I can't go back to teaching. Why did you do this to me?" When Elaine stopped to catch her breath, I tried to interrupt, but she started sobbing again.

Once I got over the initial shock of her reaction, I watched the show. The more she wailed, the more detached I felt. We were going to help her transfer into another degree program and she would keep her scholarship. She'd fare okay academically unless she made more mistakes. But in the heat of her tirade, she couldn't hear this information. I was the spectator to a magnificent hissy fit, and I haven't seen one like it since.

Surreptitiously, I checked my watch. Forty minutes later, she wound down and sat quietly. Most people calm down in twenty-five minutes or less. The challenge is not to fret over something that happened for the rest of the day and work ourselves up like Elaine.

"Now no feeling can be relied upon to last in its full intensity, or even last at all. Knowledge can last, habits can last, but feelings come and go." – C.S. Lewis

Our minds and bodies seek balance, called stasis. Our internal thermostat adjusts for hot and cold, but our body temperature remains around 98.6 degrees. Our weight fluctuates as we work to maintain a healthy balance. This is also true of our emotions. Most of us are running on anxiety and stress, not calmness. Innumerable articles and books tell us about the effects of stress and the elevated cortisol in our bodies that results. By identifying variations in our emotions, we learn to adjust and find a comfortable, consistent level.

Those with a melancholy disposition may be prone to depression. Some have problems with rage, exploding at small upsets in their routine, while others suffer from anxiety. Which emotions do you find yourself experiencing most frequently? If you experience any ongoing or uncontrolled emotional extremes, seek help.

Many people run on low levels of irritability rather than anger. Or they feel down for no obvious reason. Are you aware of your emotional balance or stasis and how it works in your life?

How we label our emotions affects how much we accept ourselves. We automatically label unpleasant emotions as "ugly" and undesirable, but they have a critical role in our lives.

Four Ugly Emotions

How do we let go of what we describe as "ugly" emotions? Again, the first step is to **Acknowledge** our painful feelings. It's easy to push them down or aside and then wonder why insomnia or stomachaches follow. We plaster a nice smile on our faces and ignore the resentment. Here are four emotions that trouble us, and our experiences with them.

ANGER

The Bible reminds us to "Be angry; and yet do not sin." Ephesians 4:26 (NASB) I've heard many people say, "I'm _____ (insert nationality here). We're known for our temper." We also act self-righteous in our anger and justify it: "Did you see what he did!? Wouldn't you be angry, too?"

The problem with anger is that it gets out of control quickly. It's easy to say or do something we later regret.

Examine your history. Did one of your parents have an explosive temper and yelled? Do you find yourself thinking, "I sound just like my mom/dad/Uncle Larry"? You didn't realize there were alternatives because this was the way everyone interacted. How on earth could you know differently?

The Bible, particularly the book of Proverbs, has multiple verses regarding anger. Here are a few:

- "A hot-tempered man stirs up strife, but the slow to anger calms a dispute." Proverbs 15:18 (NASB)
- "A soft answer turns away wrath, but a harsh word stirs up anger." Proverbs 15:1 (NKJV)
- "An angry man stirs up strife, and a furious man abounds in transgression." Proverbs 29:22 (NKJV)

Unfortunately, few of us realize we have a temper problem. Colossians 3:8 tells us we must put away anger, wrath, and malice from our mouths. What comes out, according to Jesus, exposes what's in our hearts.

If people have commented on your temper or you've hurt someone in a flash of rage, you have a problem. The solution? Find other believers who will hold you accountable, and if necessary, seek godly professional help. Consistently using the PARDA Process slows you down and identifies the triggers before you do something stupid yet again.

While I do grumble (yes, I'm working on this), I experience fewer anger blowouts. If nothing else, to keep me contained, I think about how much I hate to lose control and then apologize. Most important, I regret letting God down, then having to ask forgiveness from Him and the person I yelled at.

One experience of anger bordering on rage happened to me at a high school reunion. Guidance counselors had told me before graduation, "You can't go to college; you wear a hearing aid. You can't hear. Universities don't admit handicapped students." They didn't offer many suggestions beyond get married or find a factory job where my hearing loss didn't matter. Yes, I was hard of hearing, but not deaf. However, that made no difference.

Until the Americans with Disabilities Act in the early 1990s, many buildings were inaccessible for students with mobility issues. There were no note takers for hearing-impaired students or adjustments made for individuals with learning disabilities. Institutions could legally bar my admission because I was "handicapped." I heard about the occasional blind student who went to college, but that was rare. Usually, I was told no handicapped students went to college. Case closed.

On impulse, I took quite a number College Level Examination Program (CLEP) tests for the heck of it. Shocked, I found I had received a year of college credit. I had attended a school out of state for two semesters but couldn't afford the tuition to continue. To my delight, the University of the State of New York (not SUNY and now Excelsior College) accepted all my coursework, including two Graduate Record Exams (GRE) in specific subjects. I didn't step foot on the campus in Albany, New York, until the day before the graduation ceremony.

Looking back, it was easy to see how one small step led to another. I had no idea when I started those CLEP tests what would happen. I could *want* to succeed at these exams all I cared to, but I had to study to pass the tests. Graduate school was no different. Like undergraduate school, it took considerable time and effort that went beyond any type of wishful thinking.

At the reunion, I saw the same guidance counselor who had told me my senior year, "You can't go to college. You're handicapped." It was creepy because, like the TV star Dick Clark, he hadn't aged. I drew myself up, stood in front of him, and said, "Dr. So-and-So, you told me I couldn't go to college because I was 'deaf,' but I did. In fact, I received two master's degrees and a doctorate."

"Wow, you dumb deafies are amazing. A few of you actually succeeded," he replied.

I couldn't believe my ears. I was familiar with the pejorative expression "dumb deafies." This jerk, I mean counselor, was ignorant about what he said. He wore a big, genuine smile and acted as though he was giving me a compliment. In his eyes, he was.

"Dumb deafie" is a sarcastic yet somewhat affectionate term I heard while involved with the deaf community. Hearing this counselor with no connection to deaf individuals say those words seared my heart. Besides, I wasn't deaf, but hard of hearing. There was a difference, even if he didn't think so.

I stood there and felt rage surge through the floor into my feet and up into my chest. I couldn't catch my breath, and I began to shake. It was a challenge to use the PARDA Process in that moment. I raced through the steps in seconds.

Two or three quick breaths to **Pause**. Gingerly, I let myself **Acknowledge** the depth and intensity of my rage. I was afraid I would punch his glistening, capped teeth, so I relaxed my hands at my sides. Fortunately, I **Reflected** (and continued to breathe). Slugging a man in his late sixties? Not smart. The thought was so tempting, and I seriously considered it, but **Decided** the consequences would be too costly. Was I willing to end up in jail for assault? No, but still....

Infuriated, I **Acted** by walking away with my head held high. It took several minutes for my heart to stop racing. I later **Reflected** again on the experience and thanked my lucky stars I hadn't done anything stupid. Looking back, I wished I had said something but realized he was so clueless, there was nothing I could do. I felt bad for all the students (and their parents) harmed over the years by his condescending comments. There's no legislation against stupidity and ingrained attitudes.

Looking back over my life, I am so grateful how God opened doors for me to find jobs and attend graduate school. I'm incredibly blessed with friends and loved ones who have continued to love and accept me, warts and all. Living well is the best revenge.

FEAR

When confronted with a clear danger, our bodies react in a flash, a survival mechanism designed to protect us. Oncoming car? We swerve. Brush our fingers against a hot stove? We jerk our hands away. Immediate and specific dangers subside quickly. Sadly, many of us live with an ongoing amount of fear we label "anxiety." Lissa Rankin points out in *The Fear Cure: Cultivating Courage as Medicine for the Body, Mind and Soul*[9] how our ancestors lived far more dangerous lives. Women died in childbirth, men in battle. Nature wiped out crops or sent rains sweeping away homes. We live in a dangerous world, but in many ways, we've never been safer—far fewer women die in childbirth; since 1970, the death rate for children has dropped by more than two-thirds (pp. 122-124). Yet most of us live with a sense of ongoing anxiety, according to Rankin.

How can we deal with fear? By being in the moment, we receive practical information and guidance if we choose to heed what we think, feel, or hear. The key word here is "accurate" as in being honest with ourselves about what we think and sense.

"Fear keeps us focused on the past or worried about the future. If we can acknowledge our fear, we can realize that right now we are okay. Right now, today, we are still alive, and our bodies are working marvelously. Our eyes can still see the beautiful sky. Our ears can still hear the voices of our loved ones." – Thich Nhat Hanh

SHAME

Humans have lived in groups for many millennia. If you left your tribe, you could starve or be eaten by wild animals. Being part of a group provided protection. Guilt and shame, rightly used, kept individuals alive and close to members of their clan.

Trying to make others change their behavior by shaming them makes it worse. Teachers who document how little Johnny or Susie bit a child each day and then told the class about it learned that this "punishment" didn't improve behavior. Research shows the more shame people experience, the more aggressive and detached they become. Shame used as punishment makes things worse.

Is there an upside to shame? When we experience shame, we look inward to figure out where we screwed up. We make amends for our behavior and feel determined not to do it again.

Feelings of shame from childhood can remain with us as adults, and the associated pain can be excruciating. Growing up, I was bullied from kindergarten on because I couldn't hear. I flubbed questions in class and flubbed social interactions at lunch and recess. As I said before, people thought I was stuck up because I'd walk past them without responding to their greetings. My first hearing aid was huge despite attempts to cover it up with shoulder-length hair. It seemed a hundred times larger than the devices used today.

I dreaded a group of "in" girls who tried to toss up the hem of my dresses and chant, "I saw England, I saw France, I saw Nancy's underpants." Sometimes one girl would be kind (I thought), but a few days later, her group would surround me as their ringleader tickled and pinched me. What was more terrifying is that they tried to yank off my hearing aid. I knew it was expensive and a struggle for my parents to afford. How could I live with myself if it got damaged and my parents had to buy a new one?

Today, such behavior is unacceptable, but back then it was a part of growing up. I asked my parents for help, but their response was, "I'm sorry, sweetheart. Just ignore them, and they'll leave you alone." They tried to explain that people who hurt others were hurt down inside themselves. While I get that as an adult, hearing it while growing up was no help at all.

My teachers couldn't (or wouldn't) get involved because the behavior took place on most days just outside the wire fencing surrounding the schoolyard. Sometimes I thought I was almost home safe, then I'd be "jumped." For years I dreaded each day of school, my stomach tight and tears held back. What was wrong with me? Why was I defective? What made these girls pick on me? I felt so ashamed.

One day toward the end of seventh grade, I snapped. This time, surrounded by girls pinching me and grabbing my dress, I began to bite, scream, and kick. I felt my fist hit a face and my foot connect to someone's knee or stomach. I bit one girl's hand. My tormentors began to scream and scatter. One young girl who had wanted to be part of this group, yelled she was going to get the principal. I grabbed her arm and squeezed hard enough to leave bruises. "Yes, let's go to Dr. Adams' office." I dragged her, not caring as she tripped and fell on bits of gravel that had spilled over from the playground.

"Stop! You're hurting me!" She stared at me with terrified, tearful eyes. I felt deep disgust at my awful satisfaction from biting and kicking my tormentors. I shoved her to the ground and strode away. I was panting and didn't know if I was going to be sick. My pulse slowed as I walked home.

The next day I dreaded a call to the principal's office and a suspension. What would my parents do to me when they found out? I was terrified. But nothing happened. I was ignored. In fact, none of the girls spoke to me or came near. The next day, I waited again. After a week, I realized nothing would happen. Being ostracized wasn't so bad after years of taunting, and I welcomed the peace.

Eventually, my parents purchased a new hearing aid that was much smaller than the earlier model, thanks to the improvements in technology. My grades went up because I could hear everyone better. My relationships with a few classmates improved because I could hear more of their conversations. Then a couple of boys stopped and talked to me. Thrill, oh the thrill of that. One of them would sometimes meet me at the street crossing, and we'd walk a block to school. We lingered outside until the bell rang for class. The simple companionship gave me comfort.

"Bullying is a horrible thing. It sticks with you forever. It poisons you. But only if you let it." - Heather Brewer

Still, I felt a pervasive sense of shame at the oddest moments throughout the years. I kept asking what was wrong with me. Did

I do something to provoke the attacks? The initial surge of savage, delighted joy as I bit and kicked my tormentors made me feel worse. That meant I was no better than the bullies.

I learned compassion for myself and the children who had bullied me, and pretty much put everything behind me. It was cause for celebration when we moved, allowing me to start at a school where no one knew me.

While writing this book, I attended an out-of-state conference. On the last day, I thanked one of the hospitality ambassadors for all the work the organizers had done to make us welcome. Jane and I chatted briefly, and I learned she had attended the same grammar school, albeit a couple of years earlier than I had. To my surprise, she asked me how I felt about those years. I gave a noncommittal answer. Jane revealed how she dreaded going to school because of a group of girls who taunted her and tried to rip her clothes. She shared how she felt it was "all her fault" and her joy when she moved away because her dad changed jobs.

Then Jane told me about the mothers of those girls. These families had their own troubles. Her dad knew them well, and, without jeopardizing confidences, talked with Jane about their problems, including alcoholism, abuse, and depression. These preteens were acting out their parents' problems, although we didn't use that expression years ago.

Before we parted, Jane and I exchanged hugs and goodbyes. Old memories surged up, and I went into a bathroom stall and wept. I wept for Jane and me, the young girls who had been hurt long ago, and our tormentors. It wasn't me. I wasn't damaged or different; it had happened to others. Along with the memories, grief and shame welled up, and ultimately a sense of peace.

This story doesn't end there. Another speaker I heard later made a comment that led me to believe she and I had attended the same grammar school. Ruth, too, was a year or two older than I, and I found out she knew Jane slightly. When I mentioned the school, she blurted out, "Remember those awful girls who used to yank up other girls' dresses?" Ruth told stories of running into stores and libraries for safety until her tormentors gave up and left. Like Jane and me, Ruth had moved elsewhere with her family, and she attended a new school where no one knew her.

All three of us spoke of the shame we felt from grammar school long ago, of feeling isolated and defective. It was a time and generation when we were told, "Just ignore it and walk away." None of us confided in parents or teachers because it did no good.

Today, I feel compassion for the three of us. After what Jane had shared about the families of those girls, I hope they healed from their childhoods, as I did.

More important, I had compassion for my dark side that exploded to protect me. I wasn't an evil monster. There are times when anger *is* appropriate, and when it arises, it must be acknowledged and explored. Now when I feel anger toward another person, knowing that I have this darker side prompts self-examination. I let go of the shame. I trust these experiences make me a more loving, compassionate person.

GUILT

Unlike shame, guilt has an external focus. Our actions broke the law or violated societal norms. If possible, we try to make amends if it doesn't hurt someone else. Nasty reactions and pressure from others provide information about our actions. Society punishes people who break the law or do wrong, and guilt becomes an external tool to keep us in line. Ideally, when we experience guilt, we learn from our mistakes and vow to do better.

Guilt has been traced to what we learned as children. Parents, teachers, and authority figures try to teach us what is right and wrong with the best of intentions. Nobody wants to see a little one hurt. The issue gets cloudy, though, when a "wrong" occurs accidentally. We're wracked with guilt if our youngster gets away from us and ends up in an animal enclosure at the zoo, but it wasn't deliberate on our part.

After you **Reflect, Decide** what you will do if something similar arises again. I've been aware of the dangers of letting my anger build. When I think I'm going to say something I'll regret later, I make myself walk away. I'm also learning to examine what's underneath my anger.

Decide when and how you plan to **Act**. If you need to write a check or send a letter of apology, choose a time and date when you'll do this. Once you've made amends, what will you do when old memories arise? Some have told me after they've written letters or made amends, they take a shower and envision their transgressions swirling down the drain.

My Story: Coping with Brittany

Here's a time I used the PARDA Process on myself to get at the root of painful, tangled emotions. It's a long (and uncomfortable) story because I want to show how to use the entire process to a resolution. I wrote out my experience, thoughts and feelings around this incident.

A former classmate and I met for lunch after her husband had died earlier that year. Despite the fact Brittany lived two hours away, I attended the visitation. We had stayed connected for years by holiday cards and little else. To my surprise, she started calling me to ask questions about how to be the executor of his estate. I kept wondering why she called when she had extended family nearby.

One day, Brittany and I met for lunch. When we left the restaurant and walked to our cars, Brittany had a meltdown regarding the death of her loved one.

"Nancy, I can't stand it. I miss Jack terribly. Could you help me do the bills and talk to the lawyer? It's so hard." She cried with deep sobs and threw her arms around me, begging for help. I felt uncomfortable. When we had spoken earlier, she kept telling me "Everything is fine." With this request, I felt used and at a loss for what to do. I fell back on my training.

"You're still upset even though Jack has been gone for ten months," I said. "What is stopping you from asking for help?"

"My family doesn't do counseling," she said.

It was getting late, and I tried to extricate myself from her as Brittany sobbed, "You don't understand. It's hard." She kept sniffing into soggy tissues. Finally, we parted, and I drove home feeling drained and irritated. I felt as though I had sticky, clingy spider webs on my favorite green winter jacket. There was resentment laced with guilt for my anger and lack of sympathy. I walked around in a bookstore (a favorite form of self-therapy) and couldn't shake my mood.

I sat, **Paused,** and took slow breaths. I felt a heavy lump in my stomach and couldn't shake the sensation of spider webs on me. It was not easy to **Acknowledge** my mixed feelings of pity, anger, guilt, and sadness, let alone write about them.

Then I had to **Reflect**. The first and strongest emotion as I recalled this event was anger, and its intensity surprised me. Here I thought we were meeting as friends for lunch, but Brittany wanted free therapy. Furthermore, our relationship was superficial. We met for lunch every couple of years and exchanged holiday cards to keep in touch. So why was she calling me when she had a supportive family?

Next, I felt guilty for not being more sympathetic. I *should* feel more understanding. Instead, I felt exasperated and impatient. Nice girls shouldn't be impatient when someone is hurting, should they?

"Should" is can be a warning flag, as in, "I *should* finish the laundry before I go out to dinner." It sounds like the teacher, parent, or boss who says, "I'm telling you this for your own good. You *should...*"

After I wrote it all out, I spoke with a close friend. She asked me if I felt guilty about telling Brittany to get on with life and stop bothering me with her grief. I squirmed. What bothered me was not her grief but her telephone calls when she talked for more than an hour on weeknights when I had to go to work in the morning. When I suggested counseling because her "supportive" relatives weren't helpful, she became indignant.

I **Decided** I needed a strategy to avoid conversations on nights when I had to leave for work. I had allowed my boundaries to be violated while she spewed out intense emotions on the pretense of looking for advice. My **Actions** would include using voicemail and, because she refused to use email, I'd send a note by snail mail explaining I didn't want to return her demands to call back immediately if she didn't leave a detailed explanation.

The more I thought about what had transpired with Brittany, the more I realized my "ugly" emotions had served me well.

- My anger helped me pinpoint why I felt upset.
- My guilt kept me calm instead of snarling.
- I identified coping strategies and established boundaries.

Finally, because I had a process to deal with unpleasant emotions, I created ways to cope without guilt.

Because I took the time, the PARDA Process worked. The steps were simple; the challenge was trusting the process while allowing issues to arise without judgment.

Unresolved Guilt and Shame

If you've written about that guilt-inducing event and still experience strong emotions, or you're facing legal complications when you make amends, seek professional advice. Remaining stuck can lead to depression or cause illness. Learning from your mistakes is a healthy and necessary part of growth. It becomes unhealthy when you take your present energy and focus on the past.

A severe form of guilt and shame experienced by many military veterans is post-traumatic stress disorder (PTSD). Countries are losing thousands of vets annually to depression, despair, and suicide. As a former therapist, I know professionals are out there to help, so if you are experiencing PTSD, seek assistance.

Social media shaming exposes people's mistakes far beyond the initial event. People have lost friends, spouses, and jobs due to this online version of public shaming. Fortunately, there's starting to be a backlash. I'm meeting more and more younger millennials who are choosing to delete their social media accounts because they realize the amount of time wasted and feelings of inferiority when they view what others are doing.

"Guilt upon the conscience, like rust upon iron, both defiles and consumes it, gnawing and creeping into it, as that does which at last eats out the very heart and substance of the metal." – Robert South

Exploring and Healing Shame-based Events

My shame was painful, but I was able to take some control toward ending it. What about those who have experienced ongoing sexual abuse or exploitation? They feel a deep sense of self-revulsion, despite being told that the victim isn't to blame. I urge folks to find support groups and safe places to heal painful experiences. If you're experiencing deep, pervasive shame, seek counseling from professionals. Have compassion on yourself and find a safe place for healing.

If you have a shame-based event rattling around in your memories, stop shoving it into the back of your mind like smelly trash. Take a chance and do the PARDA Process instead. Find a quiet place where you won't be disturbed. Turn off your cell phone and other electronics. Grab a pen and pad of paper and just get writing.

For your first writing dump, I suggest you recall something that happened months or years ago. This is not the time to experiment with the intensity of a recent experience. Practice on less challenging events at first.

Pause for three or four calming breaths. Spill out a description of what happened as specifically as possible. If waves of shame well up, keep scribbling. Write more. Do at least fifteen to twenty minutes of writing and use a timer. Don't worry about any four-letter words, bad grammar, and rotten spelling. When you get stuck, repeat the last word(s) and keep going until the timer dings.

When the timer goes off, **Pause**. Do you need to write further? Go ahead. Honor yourself by writing about the pain and shame flooding your body. Thank yourself for having the courage to write about this event. Accept the shame, anger, and/or other emotions without judging yourself. Let the tears flow.

Shame versus Embarrassment

A simple definition of shame is when we've done something that violates our own inner code. For example, we don't like how we acted in a situation. We did wrong when we should have stepped up to the plate and done better. We feel inferior as a person. Shame has an interior sense and focus.

However, shame used wisely does have a purpose. When we hurt someone, we're motivated to do better in the future. Shame makes us determined to make amends and correct our mistakes.

Taken to an extreme, though, we become stuck in a loop. Then we need courage to reach out for help and get back on track.

Embarrassment, on the other hand, isn't related to feeling inherently bad and wrong. Rather, it's feeling anywhere from silly to humiliated for something inappropriate, whether it was your fault or not.

Here's an embarrassing public speaking experience, one I find rather funny in retrospect. I was doing a presentation in front of a large, affluent gathering. It was going great—until I stepped down from the podium. My long skirt caught on a nail and tore. My underwear peeked through the flimsy slip that ripped as well. Walking more than one hundred feet back to my seat while clutching the back of my skirt and slip was the longest walk I've ever taken.

Humiliated, I grabbed my coat and fled. When I reexamined the memory, I paused, breathed, and looked back at what was happening around me. I realized everyone felt sorry for me but didn't know what to say. People reacted with everything from pity to raised eyebrows to suppressed, nervous giggles. What saved me was knowing I'd never see these people again. If I have seen them since, nobody has mentioned this after-dinner debacle.

While I feel residual mortification recalling the event, I also recognize a blessing. Public speaking is not my favorite activity, but the worst happened, and the walls didn't collapse. I survived. Yes, I felt embarrassed, foolish, and stupid. But there wasn't any shame because I hadn't violated an inner ethical code. It was an unfortunate event that made me feel humiliated because I looked ridiculous. Realistically, there was no way I could have prevented my skirt from snagging on a protruding nail.

Can you have compassion for yourself? If someone came to you with this situation, what would you say? Knowing what you know now, what did you learn? Was there an upside such as being more understanding of your own and others' feelings?

Self-compassion: Be Kind to Yourself

We urge people to be compassionate and kind to everyone. But are we kind to ourselves? Brooks Palmer, the author of a delightful book on home and office organization called *Clutter Busting,* urges clients to be kind to themselves. When they spew in shame about how disorganized they are, he ignores their words and starts helping them declutter. Palmer takes an object and holds it up. "Do you want to keep this, or can you let it go?" When clients get off track, he tells them to be kind to themselves and become present in the moment.

"Three things in human life are important. The first is to be kind. The second is to be kind. And the third is to be kind." – Henry James

Sadly, we're not kind, particularly to ourselves. That's why I keep urging you to be gentle with yourself. Treat yourself like a tired toddler. Be as kind to yourself as you would be to your friends.

Paul Gilbert, founder of the Compassionate Mind Foundation and a leader in promoting compassion-based therapy, says this on his website: "The courage to be compassionate lies in the willingness to see into the nature and causes of suffering—be that in ourselves, in others and the human condition. The challenge is to acquire the wisdom we need to address the causes of suffering in ourselves and others...."[10] Humans by nature want to relieve suffering.

In his lengthy article "The Compassionate Mind Foundation and Compassion Focused Therapy"[11] reproduced from the international UK Compassionate Mind Foundation webpage, Gilbert explores a possible biological basis for compassion and altruism in the brain—along with fear, anger, sadness, and other challenges to compassion.

Many books have been written on the concept of compassion. How are we kind and compassionate to ourselves? Have you ever wallowed in praise for yourself instead of condemnation? Do you savor the joy of completing a distasteful job? Do you ever take time to appreciate yourself for doing the right thing? "Hey, you did the dishes, filed papers, and hung up your clothes. Now enjoy curling up with a murder mystery for the rest of the afternoon."

There is nothing wrong with praising yourself. Have as much fun with it as hearing friends praise and reward each other for mastering challenges and trivialities. When Maureen calls me, I get to tell her I did my writing stint today. And I'll tell her I put away the Christmas cards instead of leaving them in a holiday basket until February—well, March. It sounds silly, but it's an inexpensive reward nevertheless.

As noted earlier, being gentle with yourself during painful experiences will encourage you to be curious and explore. Instead of running and avoiding discomfort, allow it into your life. Shame and guilt are useful if you learn from the experiences that caused you to feel them. While it's scary to **Pause** and let unpleasant feelings go through your body, you're then free to decide what to do next. Your heart and mind are in harmony.

Realize that self-compassion doesn't mean wallowing in self-pity. When we remind ourselves "we'll get through this" or "others have similar problems," it becomes easier to let go. The word here is "gently."

"People who are brutally honest get more satisfaction out of the brutality than out of the honesty." – Richard J. Needham

Do you take pride in "telling it like it is"? Is this helpful? I'm afraid if I'm kind to myself, I'll become lazy and careless. I need to crack the whip and kick myself around or nothing will get done. Is it possible let go of the need to be strong, to have a "stiff upper lip" no matter what life throws at you?

Acknowledge is an opportunity to explore pain, anger, or upset—without judgment—and move on. This isn't being weak. It's being human and brave. When you **Acknowledge** without judgment your unpleasant experiences, feeling the momentary flood of shame or anger, the emotions will pass. You stop avoiding painful memories because they feel too painful to examine.

Research has shown the harm that results when people shame themselves and others. "I can't believe I screwed up," you tell yourself. Step back. Own what happened and your role in it. Consider this approach instead: "I screwed up by inserting the wrong figures in the departmental report. I feel awful. But I will figure out how to get the numbers sooner. I will find someone to proofread the report before it's sent."

Compassion toward both yourself and others isn't being wimpy. It's not condoning or minimizing poor behavior. Toxic responses are things like berating others' choices or thinking they're stupid. Compassion for yourself and others means you accept that all of us make mistakes.

Psychologist Kristen Neff notes in her book *Self-Compassion: The Proven Power of Being Kind to Yourself*[12] that while we have compassion for others, it's far more difficult to be kind to ourselves. She recounts her own struggles to treat herself with kindness. Think about it: we treat ourselves far more harshly than we treat our friends. When we screw up, good friends give us a hug and help us move on. Why can't we do that for ourselves? Doing one small move again and again takes the pressure off. We learn to step back and stop treating ourselves harshly. Tiny steps work.

When we are kind to ourselves we develop courage to look at the truth of our emotions and their results. At the end of the day, we want to look ourselves in the mirror without shame or judgment as we get ready for bed.

One of my professors in grad school made a comment that has stayed with me: "We're all doing the best we can. Even when others' actions seem maladaptive or harmful, people are doing the best they can with what they know."

Personal Vulnerability

It's hard enough to be vulnerable in front of others, but I'm shocked at how hard it is for me to be vulnerable with myself. The old quote, "Character is who you are when no one's looking," describes my struggle. How do I face my flaws when I'm alone with me, much less within my journal?

Or do I go to the opposite extreme—that is, accept and embrace my dark side? I have detailed mental list of all my faults. My friends and husband (I'm convinced) would gladly add to them if asked! It's as though we want to flaunt our dark side as another badge next to the one we wear to show off our overbooked lives.

"When you really need help, people will respond. Sincerity means dropping the image façade and showing a willingness to be vulnerable....ask from your heart. Keep it simple, and people will open up to you." – Jack Canfield

Most of us avoid being vulnerable in front of others because we're terrified of what people think of us. Brené Brown, who pioneered the research on shame and vulnerability, notes that men and women express shame differently. Women are supposed to be quiet and "nice." Men are to be stoic and do well at work and life. Brown challenges us to take appropriate risks and be true to who we are in related circumstances. In her opinion (and I agree), shame is one of the most toxic emotions we experience. Shame, and the fear of being vulnerable, make it hard for us to be ourselves, especially during tough circumstances.

Psychology has the concept of the "shadow," which refers to the parts of us we're reluctant to accept or recognize exist. You know, it's the petty glee we repress when a rival makes a mistake in front of the entire department. Or consider the perfect profile on Facebook that doesn't mention unpleasant events. Or notice the parts we've shoved aside for years because they're too shameful to examine.

While there's a dark side of our personality, we also squelch the creative and "better" parts of our psyche. Carl Jung, a pioneer in psychology, labels this the "golden shadow."

My friend Pat had studied Jungian psychology. In addition to operating a private therapy practice, she took stunning photographs and showed them at art fairs. Our times together were full of laughter and vulnerability to each other. I loved visiting her elegantly decorated home and studio. It amazed me to see her works in progress as she matted and framed photos. Sometimes she had to sift through dozens of them before she found the "perfect" image. She didn't care how much time she took taking multiple shots to capture the right image.

Pat showed me how she experimented with assorted colors and how one change made a picture "pop." The dozens of useless shots she took? That was a part of the process. One day, Pat looked me straight in the eye. "Nancy, you wouldn't be drawn to my house and studio if you weren't an artist yourself at some level." I stared.

"Toddlers draw better stick figures than do," I told her. "Who are you kidding?"

"You're thinking in terms of photography and painting. You have other gifts—soul qualities you're afraid to show people," she told me. She referred to my creative side that I was too scared to acknowledge. Most painful of all, she added, "You will not be a whole person, walking in honesty, if you don't own those loving, creative parts of who you are."

Pat passed on several years ago, but I continue to reflect on her words and challenge. I was blessed by her willingness to affirm me, flaws and virtues without judgment.

Turning to God

Being vulnerable in front of others is challenging and coming before God even more so. In our feelings regarding any wrongdoing, we can turn to God and ask His forgiveness for a specific situation. Again, John 1:9 reminds us that if we admit to God we have sinned, He forgives us. God forgave King David when he repented of his sin and confessed it to the Lord in Psalm 32:5: "I acknowledged my sin to You, and my iniquity I have not hidden. I said, 'I will confess my transgressions to the Lord,' and You forgave the iniquity of my sin." (NKJ) This is from a man who committed adultery, then murdered the husband to cover up his affair.

Many of us believe we should get "cleaned up" and put ourselves together before we ask God for forgiveness and help. Not true. Most of the time, what stops us from turning to Him is pride—that is, having to admit we can't do it ourselves and we're sinners. We want to turn to God on *our* terms, not His.

America is a land of immigrants. People need a deep level of courage and desperation to go to a strange country where they don't know anyone to start a new life. Many must learn a new language and start from nothing. Consequently, America glorifies individualists more than other cultures. Here a few of many ways this trait appears:

- A "Declaration of Independence."
- Poems like *Invictus* telling us we are the "master of our fate, the captain of our soul."
- Songs like *I'll Do It My Way.*
- Heroes like the cowboys and pioneers in *Bonanza* and *Little House on the Prairie.*
- Rags-to-riches stories by Horatio Alger.

Submit to God? His will? You've got to be kidding. Forgiveness? Not going there, thank you very much. How could I ever forget what so-and-so did to me? Revenge feels sweet.

I hear you ask, "Do you know how many times I would have to turn to God during the day?" That's okay.

Being in a relationship with God in some ways is like being married or valuing a close friend. You work at making sure the lines of communication stay open. You admit when you made a mistake or said something that hurt your loved one.

None of this is easy. Some days I'm thinking, "God, I'm trying to be polite, but it's the last thing I want to do. Please forgive me." Or, "Lord, I'm struggling to keep my lips sealed and not make the nasty remarks I'm thinking right now." I've been there many times and will likely be in that ditch again. It's tempting to try to hide from God and pretend nothing happened. Try this instead:

Pause before the Lord for a few minutes.

Acknowledge specifically what you have done before God and ask His forgiveness. Remind yourself of 1John 1:9, that if we confess our sins, God forgives us.

Reflect about what you wrote. Step back and see yourself as you once were. When I reread my notes, I see a scared little girl who yearned for acceptance instead of a stupid kid wearing a large, expensive hearing aid her parents struggled to afford. Now I recall classmates who reached out to me, but back then, we depended on our parents to drive us to each other's homes for visits. I did attend a few birthday parties, which meant I wasn't as alone as I thought.

Sharing Your Dark Places with God

No matter how much I explore disturbing emotions and experiences, there are times when I still feel a deep sense of unworthiness and shame. Most of us struggle with strong emotions of shame and guilt as we acknowledge our shortcomings. It's painful to realize God already knows us. We can't hide from Him, no matter how hard we try. Read Psalm 139. God knows us intimately.

Read Romans, Chapter 7. Paul states that when he wants to do good, he can't, and does what's wrong even though he doesn't want to. He's upset and angry. But there's nothing he can do. In fact, the harder he tries, the worse it gets.

But the God who knows us and our shortcomings still loves us. Romans 8, starting at the first verse, brings staggering, joyful news: Despite Paul's flaws and our own, Paul writes, "Therefore, there is now no condemnation for those who are in Christ Jesus." (NASB) By sending His Son, Jesus Christ, to die for us and pay the price for our sins, God wiped out our sin forever with Christ's blood.

Daily, I need to claim 1 John 1:9, where it is written, "If we confess our sins, He is faithful and just to forgive us our sins and to cleanse us from all unrighteousness." (NKJV) As a follower of Jesus Christ who has these promises available, it makes it far easier for me to turn to God when I screw up, which seems like multiple times each hour some days.

All of us have parts of our personality called the "shadow self" that we're ashamed to own. The more we stuff down our unacceptable parts, the more they'll intrude at awkward moments when we'd rather be at our best.

Writing down nasty feelings without censorship allowed me to be honest. That meant thoughts could arise without my beating myself up for not feeling as though I "should" be more caring and nicer. It took more strength than I had to be "nice" during these times.

Since I wrote my innermost feelings for me and no one else saw them, I experienced relief. I could be true to myself in the moment and didn't have to tell anyone else. Fortunately, I'm blessed with friends with whom I share my dark spaces. These friends are far kinder to me than I am to myself. I also bring these feelings to God and ask for healing by examining my thoughts and figure out (with His help) how to resolve them.

Acknowledging the less honorable parts of my personality is hard. I like to think I'm a good person. I don't like to admit how much drivers irritate me or that I'm envious of a friend's new home. When I do decide to recognize these thoughts, however, in their raw intensity, they subside. It's easier to step back. I ask God for His forgiveness as I forgive others and start the healing.

When I was honest about my "bad" feelings, I felt heard deep in my soul. I no longer shushed myself internally in much the same way my parents did to me as a child. "Oh, honey, you don't hate Mrs. So-and-So." (But in that instant, I did hate her.) It took years as an adult to be willing to accept my dark side with self-compassion. Once anger or dislike or hurt arises in my heart, I go to God and tell him He needs to give me the love or caring I need.

When you acknowledge an event or circumstance, be honest with yourself, regardless of whether you tell someone else or not.

Come to Your Senses and Move Forward

Once the initial shock of reflection is over, you come to your senses and look inward at what happened. Because of the experience, you then **Decide** on changes.

Once I have decided with God's help what changes need to occur, I explore how to **Act** when similar temptations and situations arise again. How I wish this was a once-and-for-all experience. I still struggle with flaws and continue to experience the push-pull of doing what I don't want to do as Paul described in Romans, Chapter 7.

I am grateful God doesn't condemn me in my struggles with sin—a struggle I will have until I'm home in Heaven. I do know this: People may hurt or betray me, but God loves me anyway.

Chapter 5

What Are You Telling Yourself?

When you're alone, be honest in your mind. Ask yourself if a change is something you truly want, or does it stem from past experiences that are no longer relevant today. First, we'll identify some unhealthy ways we deal with self-talk and endless thought loops. Then we'll explore ways to adjust our self-talk and make changes. Listen to your internal chatter for clues on how to stop sabotaging yourself.

Self-talk Arguments That Go Nowhere

How many times a day do you argue with yourself? Some of us do this with food. "That chocolate cake looks luscious. See that vanilla ganache frosting. I can't disappoint my sister after she spent all day cooking this great meal." You think about the rich frosting, and that's when you've lost the battle. You have "just a little sliver" and end up taking a huge slab of cake home with you.

We debate whether we should do something now or later. It's easy to rationalize not doing the dishes or paperwork until later, then feel exasperated with our procrastination.

When we argue inside our heads, we lose the battle. We selectively edit the internal discussion without realizing it, and afterwards, we beat ourselves up. Later in the book, we'll discuss action strategies, but for now, write down the habitual dialog going on inside your head. Once you see it on paper, you'll roll your eyes at the content—but do it anyway.

"Self-talk reflects your innermost feelings." - Asa Don Brown

"Yeah, but …"

One of many voices is the one that finds excuses why something won't work. My dad had a habit of talking himself in and out of ideas. "Wouldn't it be great to get a new car?" He'd be excited, but then his thoughts would ramble.

"Yeah, but the old car is in pretty good shape."

"I don't know if I want to be saddled with car payments."

"Yeah, but selling it now means we'd have more to put down for the new car."

"I could sell it to Fred down the street."

"But if it breaks down, he'll be upset, and I'll feel guilty for selling him my old clunker."

Mentally, he argued back and forth with himself. I figured out this was one way he made decisions. All I knew is when we heard these conversations at the dinner table, it was best to wait him out rather than intervene.

 We all have an internal dialogue. "Yeah, I want to work on my term paper, but since I don't have enough research, I'll do it later." "Yeah, I need to do laundry, but I don't have enough for a full load."

I used to believe those "yeah, but" statements were a form of procrastination. It meant I'd better ignore them and buckle down to work. Then I found myself stalling again. Are these "buts" procrastination or was something else going on? As Freud said, "Sometimes a cigar is just a cigar." Maybe there's no deeper meaning to your "yeah, but" thoughts.

Pause and breathe for a moment or two. Where do you experience the resistance of the "yeah, but" in your body? Your stomach? Chest? Shoulders?

Acknowledge this resistance. Let it be there. Be mildly curious. What thoughts are coming up? Grab your notebook or a piece of paper and start writing. Regarding the term paper, is your body telling you that you don't have enough information? Or you don't have a suitable topic for this assignment? Are these legitimate concerns and obstacles? Wait it out, or better still, write it out. What feeling comes up? I'll bet you dollars to donuts it's fear. It can be fear of failure or not being good enough. It could be countless other fears.

Do you see how your brain is a fertile source of fears masquerading as excuses?

Reflect on the fears you wrote down. Be gentle with yourself. Comfort your scared internal kid who's terrified of letting you and the world down. Those "yeah, buts" are an attempt by your psyche, your unconscious mind, to protect you from danger. But here's the thing: You're an adult. Do your best to protect your internal, scared child from harm, despite life being too uncertain for ironclad guarantees.

It's April, and you're terrified about doing your taxes. You might have legitimate concerns, since you're not sure of the right forms. From the beginning you've felt a nagging fear there's an error, but you can't find it. Honor your anxiety and explore your options. Just be sure you don't ignore or stifle those fears without examining them first.

Decide on your first small step and begin. Work on the first page for ten minutes, then walk away. "But how am I going to get this done?" your inner child sputters. "It's due in three days." If previous efforts to ram it through have failed, you have nothing to lose by experimenting. Decide you'll come back in half an hour and work for another twenty minutes, but no longer. Deliberately slow down and focus on one line at a time. Paradoxically, you will increase your desire to finish because you forced yourself to stop. To your surprise, a few hours later you discover a miscalculation that once corrected, makes all the numbers come out correctly.

Act by making a tiny step. When do you plan to return to your taxes? What will you for the ten minutes? During the thirty minutes you walk away, will you drink a bottle of water or play your flute? Write down additional ideas.

Keep moving in tiny steps until you're finished. Yes, it seems to take forever, but sitting there and arguing in your head doesn't work. Get moving instead.

Accepting the Voices

Mostly, I've reached the point of taking a deep breath, then describing what's happening inside without judgment. To my surprise, I realized that often the voice is that of a small child who's terrified at what will happen because she made a simple mistake. Memories of adults in my life who yelled at me came flooding back. Today, I realize it's me, one terrified little kid, and I'm doing it to myself.

But if I hadn't spent time accepting this yappy, high-pitched voice without judgment (I find myself saying, "Oh, yappy's back"), I wouldn't have discovered the source. The voice is a trigger that lets me know I'm scared. As the adult, I step back and assess if there's a reason to be frightened. Most of the time, there isn't. Still, this poor inner kid is trying to protect me from getting clobbered. I need to address worries, then find comfort for both of us. Bit by bit, it gets easier.

If you were dealing with a scared toddler, would you yell and spank for being upset? Your internal toddler can't run your life. Yes, she should be acknowledged and comforted. But would you give a four-year-old the keys to your car? Your adult self can comfort and nurture this scared childlike part while maintaining control of a situation. Thank this little one for all her hard work in trying to help you with the best of intentions.

It's fascinating how people describe their inner child voices once they coax them out. Most of us express guilt about how poorly we've treated this part of our personality. On the one hand, this little kid wants to protect us from harm, while on the other, it has driven us to spend money or engage in inappropriate relationships based on misguided intentions. We'll explore how to work with our inner voices and turn them into our allies.

Rework Your Voices

Once you have reached the point where you can compassionately accept what you're saying to yourself, decide how you want to change your words without necessarily getting rid of them. Science-based research is showing ways to use our inner voices to our advantage. I found several ways to challenge my interior monologue once I began exploring what I heard.

For example, who is telling "you" the various commands disguised as suggestions? Is it a reflection of an earlier voice of authority?

- "I/You should be more organized."
- "I/You need to be going to the gym."
- "I/You must get caught up on my/your paperwork."

Using phrases that start with "I should," "I must," or "I have to" is nagging at best and shaming at worst. These kinds of phrases don't work with others, so why are you saying them to yourself?

If you can't bring yourself to stop using these phrases, then at least change them to the third person and use the word "could". This gives you a choice. There's something about being told you *have* to do something that spins you right back to childhood. It's like being told to clean your room when you'd rather play.

It's fascinating to monitor all the chatter going on in our minds. "Finish this report for work." "I wonder if we're going out this weekend or staying inside." "Oh yikes, why did I do that?" It's not necessary to wallow within the chatter, but when we examine what's going on beyond a triggering event, we gather information.

This is especially true when we're in the grip of strong emotions such as joy, anger, and sorrow. We know from anatomy and physiology about a part of the brain called the amygdala. This small, nut-sized organ is on the alert for danger. "Look, is that a lion?" "What was that rustle?" "Who's there?" This alertness kept our ancestors alive over the millennia. When the amygdala is on overdrive, we're tense and expect the worst. We struggle to soothe ourselves.

Taming our brains and bodies is a challenge. Health experts warn us to reduce our blood pressure and lower our stress levels. With God's help, step back from alarming situations.

What would happen if we spoke back to those internal voices without being nasty? Instead of, "Boy, was that stupid," we'd say, "Daniel, try doing the report a week earlier. When will you start?" Performing multiple small acts of compassion for ourselves is healing.

"You find out what you think by talking to yourself." – Robert Harris

The challenge is to figure out exactly what we're thinking in the moment. One workaround is to figure out what part of the body is clamoring for attention. If it could talk, what would it say? Write down your thoughts, no matter how trivial. That way, you'll examine the emotional flavor of the words without judgment.

Talk to Yourself in Third Person

I discovered talking to myself in the third person distances me from an upset. I'd say, "Nancy, you're scared about the speech. Why not start by writing notes about what you want to say? Better, find a place where you won't be heard and talk to yourself. Who cares if it's stupid? Your racing thoughts will slow down. Think of the classic British mysteries when the heroine says out loud to herself, "Buck up, old girl."

Recent research supports the positive effects of talking to yourself in the third person rather than using "I." It's called self-distancing. I didn't know that when I started my self-talk; all I knew was how much better I felt when I did it. According to performance psychologist Noa Kageyama, Ph.D., third-person self-talk reduces shame, anxiety, and rumination. In his blog post at the Bullet Proof Musician[13] he notes research supporting the idea that third-person self-talk improves performance. He advocates keeping self-talk to yourself, so you won't disturb others.

Michala Chung, author of *The Irresistible Introvert: Harness the Power of Quiet Charisma in a Loud World*,[14] noted that when you can't obtain validation from someone else, an internal voice speaking in the third person works as a soothing replacement. She learned (like me) from her experience about the helpfulness of second- or third-person self-talk, then found the research to validate her experience. Chung mentioned research from psychologist Ethan Kross, who also found that talking to yourself in the first person as "I" is less effective than speaking in third person.[15] The process lets us gain emotional distance and self-control, which allows us to think more clearly. Just as we see our friends' problems better than our own, third-person self-talk has a similar effect.

A study from *Scientific Reports* found comparable results. Silently talking to yourself in the third person might constitute a form of self-control. The researchers hypothesized that it does, since third-person self-talk leads people to think about the self similarly to how they think about others. This, in turn, provides them with the psychological distance for self-control.[16]

A good place for affirmative, third-person self-talk is talking aloud in the car with the windows rolled up. It also works in the shower with the water running. When you're home, close the door and turn on a radio or TV. The sounds mask your voice, and others won't hear what you're saying.

Use Your Own Phrases and Comfort Words

When I use affirmations, I keep hearing this little voice say, "Who are you kidding?" Affirmations don't fit my personality. But if you find them useful, keep saying them. While I don't use affirmations as such, I find certain words and phrases are helpful and I turn to them as a resource when I'm under stress.

When things turn rough, I find myself mumbling aloud. "We'll get through this. We *will* get through this. I'm not sure how, but we'll get through this." By the grace of God, I always do. Looking back on a few of the rough patches, I don't how or where I found the strength.

That isn't a bad internal resource to have, is it?

We laugh at the proliferation of signs saying, "Keep calm and carry on," but it's a powerful message. What phrases can you use in your life? What about:

- "Keep going for a few minutes longer."
- "I'm not scared, maybe just excited."
- "Others have succeeded, and I will, too."

Hang on to these and similar phrases, and then recall and repeat them to get you through a crunch. (In Appendix B, you'll find a list called "What to Say to Yourself When It's All Falling Apart.")

Dialogue with Your Thoughts

Psychologists Hal and Sidra Stone, founders of Voice Dialogue at http://delos-inc.com, developed a process to engage with the many selves that make up one's personality, that we experience as inner voices. All of us have roles in life. The goal is to integrate those roles and make them internally consistent. At work I dress conservatively, while at home I run around in old jeans and baggy sweatshirts. Maybe I could loosen up my attire at work and be less grungy at home. My clothes illuminate my roles and personality.

Dialoging lets you **Acknowledge** all the distinct parts of you in your head that argue about a problem or course of action. Begin by giving them names and allow them to speak. The more descriptive, the better. I discovered that I have a Stuffy Banker who's great for curbing my internal impulsive spender, and the internal Work Horse focuses me to finish distasteful jobs. The Wordsmith is my writing self.

These parts argue with each other. The Wordsmith is aggravated with the Work Horse and Stuffy Banker because they try to smother my writing efforts. They insist their needs come first.

What fascinated Hal and Sidra Stone, along with their trainees, is how the most strident, obnoxious voices have good intentions. My Stuffy Banker is fearful I'll overspend, end up in debt, and become a homeless bag lady. When I spend buy a book or a cup of hot chocolate at the bookstore, I think I should justify my splurge. But these aspects negotiated a truce and agreed I could incorporate book-writing time and chocolate dates into my budget.

We're all happier with each other now. The Banker honors my caution and the Wordsmith is rewarded for her writing efforts. The Workhorse has a chance to relax for once. Thank your parts, for all your good intentions.

Once you have written out the dialogue, it's easier to keep a journal of observations. Write down whose voice it is. Is it loud? Encouraging? Does it help you?

It is tempting to answer these questions inside your head. Don't. Write down your answers and engage your voices. Be curious. What are they saying and what do you learn from them?

"That was really stupid of you."

"So, who asked you?"

"How could you have forgotten your car keys AGAIN. Can't you be better organized?" (I wonder whose voice this is. It seems familiar, but I can't recognize it.)

"You're right, I did forget my car keys in my jeans when I walked out the door. But it happens only once or twice a year. Besides, I've got a spare in my purse."

"You SHOULD be more organized. What if you lose your work keys? Or get locked out of the house or your car late at night?"

When I listen to this strident voice, I recognize an aunt's words from my childhood who was blamed for not being more organized. According stories I heard growing up, she ran the household after her mother died when she was fourteen years old. So, I say, *"Aunt Linda, thank you for trying to help me be organized. But I'm a big girl now, and it's okay to leave me alone."*

Despite my irritation, she has a point. I honor her concern by making sure I have additional keys stashed in case I need them. Furthermore, my friends and I have exchanged keys in case we go out of town or lose them.

Funny thing, when a similar situation happened, I recognized the Aunt Linda voice behind my eyeballs. It was muted, but I used it as an internal check-in without beating myself up, and I'll continue to do so. She serves a purpose.

We think we need to eliminate all the old tapes running inside our heads. It's like trying to deal with an annoying sound by ignoring it. Wouldn't it be better to turn the sound down without turning it off completely?

By choosing to lower the emotional volume, we retain the memories and what we've learned from them. The emotional charge is gone, and we acknowledge the intention of the voices to protect us.

When we **Reflect** on experiences from the past with our emotions in the present, we begin to unravel memories and tapes from childhood. We forget that as young children we believe adults rule the world. What they tell us, right or wrong, is the absolute truth. For the most part, the adults in our lives had good intentions. But, there comes a time to evaluate what we've heard and learned. Does the information serve us today? Or must we reassess the validity of an internal perception?

The challenge is working with the insights enough to motivate us to change. We know what we're doing is wrong or stupid, but we lack the tools to make a course correction. How do we take action?

We've talked it out and written it down, but what if the memories and voices refuse to fade? Studies have shown asking people to relive painful events such as shootings or traffic accidents right after they've happened isn't helpful. In fact, doing so makes things worse for some individuals. Do get help if the PARDA Process or other self-help ideas don't work.

What Do Others Say to You?

When you **Acknowledge** your internal thoughts and emotions, be sure to include what others may be saying or doing. Listening to criticism is painful because you want to be loved and accepted unconditionally.

Once you **Pause**, step back and **Acknowledge** what you heard. Look at this as an opportunity to learn. Are the comments legitimate? The old saying "consider the source" applies here. The acquaintance or stranger who says you're stupid makes you feel uncomfortable, but the sensation leaves when you consider the source.

What if the hurtful comments come from a friend or loved one? A boss? A spouse? Again, breathe. **Pause** and **Acknowledge**. Is there any truth buried within the criticism? When you **Acknowledge** your own behavior, **Reflect** on what others said to you. Do you focus on those few words of minor criticism and ignore praises and kudos? Are people in a bad mood and taking it out on you? We beat ourselves up for not doing better when we did the best we could in the moment.

Ruminating

Have you ever seen cows resting in a field? After chowing down on their food for the day, they bring it up again to chew and re-chew it. This is called ruminating. It's peaceful for cows but not for us.

For humans, ruminating means letting the voices in your head replay endlessly. You find yourself revisiting painful conversations, and you keep beating yourself up emotionally. If you're already sad, thinking about sad topics reinforces the pain caused by your sadness.

"One reason most people never stop thinking is that mental frenzy keeps us from having to see the upsetting aspects of our

lives...I can avoid contemplating little issues like, say, my own mortality." – Martha Beck

The PARDA Process tools are for those humiliating events replaying in your head when you can't sleep at 2:00 a.m. You come up with all the sharp, witty comments you could have made. Or you remember in vivid color when someone ripped you to shreds in front of friends and coworkers. If your ruminating thoughts become overwhelming to the point that you contemplate harming yourself, please seek help immediately.

Cognitive therapy is a wonderful tool. It helps us identify painful or disturbing thoughts and dispute them. For many of us, however, bringing up those painful thoughts and emotions to dispute them makes them worse. It's as though we're on the lookout for negativity. We're too wide awake to go back to sleep, but we tell ourselves we're too tired to get up and write down the nonsense. As we argue back and forth in our head, we become more tired yet more wide awake. Does this sound familiar?

At this point, **Pause**. Use these loops to **Acknowledge** the futility of your endless thoughts. This is when I take out my notepad, pen, and a small light to illuminate the page. I jot down a few words and calm down. Things always look better in the morning.

One way to minimize these late-night ruminations is to take time at the end of the day to recall what happened. When we use those few moments to step away, we **Reflect** on the day's activities and sort them out. What went right? If something went wrong, what did we learn? What will you do differently? Write down your thoughts and fall asleep. It will be there in the morning.

Meditate, Not Ruminate

When I discuss the idea of incorporating pauses in one's life, people jump to the idea of meditation. Hackles rise. Phrases pop up such as, "I don't have time to sit and stare at nothing." I've been surprised at the level of defensiveness on the topic.

But what if I told you there's a different way to meditate? **Reflect**, which is one of the steps in the PARDA Process, is a type of meditation found throughout the Bible. Joshua is told to meditate on God's word day and night (Joshua 1:8). Psalm 1:2 describes the righteous person whose "...delight is in the law of the Lord, and on his law he meditates day and night." (ESV)

Meditation used this way is a form of focused thinking that keeps intrusive thoughts at bay. If used regularly, it will reduce ruminating. There's another benefit, too.

When we saturate our minds in God's word, it begins to change us at deeper levels. Philippians 4:8 urges: "Whatever is true, whatever is honorable, whatever is right, whatever is pure, whatever is lovely, whatever is of good repute, if there is any excellence and if anything worthy of praise, dwell on these things." (NASB) In a time when we're flooded with unsavory news, we need to choose where to place our focus.

"Take everything easy and quit dreaming and brooding and you will be well guarded from a thousand evils." – Amy Lowell

I've described how much my mind races 24/7. When I'm in the dentist's chair, my mind and body flood with anxiety and upsetting thoughts. I tense when the chair is tilted, and the assistant drapes the paper bib. My dentist is skillful, and the pain minimal, but terrifying childhood memories of earlier dental visits remain. Whether it's a simple cleaning or the nip of the needle that grants blessed numbness, my body braces itself. My mind and pulse both race, and I struggle to slow my breathing.

This is when memorized scripture verses have helped. A verse I cling to every time I head for the dentist is from Isaiah 41:10: "Fear thou not; for I am with thee: be not dismayed; for I am thy God: I will strengthen thee; yea, I will help thee; yea, I will uphold thee with the right hand of my righteousness." (KJV)

I force myself to slow my breathing and focus on relaxing my tight muscles. Again, I repeat to myself, "Fear thou not, for I am with thee..." I mindfully repeat various verses multiple times until the procedure is over.

Another helpful verse is Ephesians 6:14: "...and having done everything, to stand firm." (NASB) Sometimes all I can do in the middle of a crisis is to stay put and cling to God in trust, having no clue what's happening or what lies ahead. I remain in His Presence, holding on as my world crashes around me. It's like a song repeating in my head, but as I focus on the verse, I am soothed and at peace.

First thing in the morning and the last thing at night, I try to make it a point to be thinking about a verse. When I awaken, I think or say, "This is the day which the Lord hath made; we will rejoice and be glad in it." Psalm 118:24 (KJV) There are too many days, however, when saying this verse is an act of will, rather than based on happy feelings. Then I use habit to get me going.

Lying in bed at night, I thoughtfully repeat the Lord's Prayer ("Our Father") or a phrase such as "Be still and know that I am God." The challenge with these practices is to do them with focus. This is the opposite of the "mindless repetition" described in Matthew 6:7.

During the day, I think about something from the Scriptures I've read earlier or heard in a sermon. I connect the thought with additional Bible verses, or a practical application. Actions like these keep my mind focused on good things rather than brooding over the past. I ask God for guidance and do the best I can.

Making time to saturate your mind in the words of the Old and New Testament starts to refocus your heart. You begin to desire to do what is right, which conflicts with other desires. "For the word of God is living and active and sharper than any two-edged sword, and piercing as far as the division of soul and spirit, of both joints and marrow, and able to judge the thoughts and intentions of the heart." Hebrews 4:12 (NASB). Here is the real source of power for changing your life.

This shift to focusing upon Scriptures has slowly reduced my tendency towards endless rumination.

Self-Trust

When we were children, we blurted out what we were thinking and feeling. "Mommy, I hate you!" Mom says, "Oh, no you don't. Don't say such mean things that aren't true." In that instant, we did hate Mom. Yet five minutes later, the storm had blown over and we were giggling and playing.

"Be a good animal, true to your instincts." – D. H. Lawrence

When you're told over and over that your thoughts and emotions are wrong, you'll find it difficult to trust yourself. By pausing and acknowledging, you re-establish the connection to what you are feeling and hearing. Think how you receive information. We hear the words, then we see the images or experience physical sensations. This is your own input, not someone else's assessment.

Introverts like me struggle with trusting themselves. Extroverts are the desirable norm in American culture, and we force ourselves to fit in. We're ashamed to admit we enjoy being home on Saturday night with a book rather than jammed hip-to-shoulder in a crowded room. It's hard to validate our experiences if we feel ashamed for not fitting in.

Take it a step further and ask your gut what it's sensing. Scientists have found we have a second "brain" in our stomach. We've all had the "butterflies" before a major presentation or the "mmm, that doesn't feel right" sensation, but we don't quite know why. Those physiological sensations are clues. Just because we don't have a clear image or auditory cue doesn't mean they aren't valid.

All these thoughts slide into the next section of the PARDA Process, **Reflect**.

Chapter 6

Reflect

By now you have taken time to **Pause** and **Acknowledge** what you are sensing in the moment. You've learned (I hope) that your feelings aren't the end of your story. Take the next step and think about what you've discovered and what it means to you. Going forward, as we explore options, try on different ideas for implementing change and meeting goals. Reflecting first, and then deciding how you'll carry out your plans, challenges you to commit—or not.

Webster's dictionary says one definition of *reflect* is to recognize or consider. When we **Acknowledge**, we tell ourselves the story of what happened and the emotions along with it without judgment and condemnation. By contrast, when we **Reflect**, we explore what happened and assess our thoughts and feelings *about* and around the event itself.

Hundreds of years ago, people didn't have more time to think than they do now. Most tasks, however, were monotonous and allowed time for pondering. Cleaning the stables, doing laundry by hand, and planting crops allowed the mind to daydream. You had to focus enough to get the job done, but you could also think about issues or reflect on a conversation. Our ancestors sat around the fire and told stories passed down through generations. When they returned to planting their crops or curing animal hides, they recalled what they had heard around the fire. The legends that guided families and tribes were a source of comfort and strength.

"By three methods we may learn wisdom: First, by reflection, which is noblest; Second, by imitation, which is easiest; and third by experience, which is the bitterest." – Confucius

Today, we're afraid to be alone in our heads, in our bodies, or at home. The advent of social media has made it easier to distract ourselves, making the **Reflect** step difficult. This is why I stressed in the **Acknowledge** section to avoid self-condemnation. Observe yourself. What was going on before you whipped out your phone or tablet to check something online? Suddenly it became urgent to check email or social media than focus on an unsettling event. Force yourself to write for a few minutes and diffuse the upheaval. While it feels painful to focus, writing down facts and feelings shortens the process and short-circuits endless ruminating.

We're learning as a society how using the internet for ideas has hampered our ability to ponder deeply and devise our own solutions. I know I'm tempted to skim multiple articles rather than read two or three articles in detail, because thinking followed by action is hard work. It's better to take miniscule steps. This doesn't fit in view of how most of us prefer to solve our problems. Impatient, we want immediate and easy answers. We wonder why everything seems to take forever.

We think we have no time to recall events of the day or to ponder our thoughts and emotions. Instead of taking a few moments each day to look back, we rush around, do chores, eat dinner, and get ready for the next day. Families with children have additional responsibilities. With everything on our minds, we awaken in the middle of the night and can't go back to sleep. We recall unkind words, or whether we can pay the bills. That kind of reflection is painful and accomplishes little.

What It Means to Reflect

If we're honest, we're terrified to be by ourselves, let alone with our thoughts. I still insist people write down the simplest phrases, misspellings and all. When the "bad" thoughts get on paper, they lose much of their power.

When you **Reflect** on events and what you're feeling, avoid using the word "why" as in, "Why was I so stupid?" "Why doesn't he call?" When you were a teenager and your parents asked, "Why did you do that?" Your automatic response was, "Gee, I dunno." Asking "why?" is usually ineffective, which is why (pun intended) I suggest you avoid it.

I suppose there's a valid place for those kinds of questions, but they are usually endless loops going nowhere. Instead, ask questions such as, "What was happening just before I lost my temper?" "When do I find myself grabbing a bag of barbeque-flavored potato chips?" "Are there any patterns?"

Again, get in the habit of scribbling notes in your PARDA Process journal to capture your thoughts, or write on scraps of paper to dump in your PARDA notebook when you get home. Once you've done that, take a few moments and examine what you wrote. Innovative ideas and connections will appear and "aha" moments will "click" as you connect the dots.

By the way, also ask, "What went right?" It's tempting to get into what therapists call catastrophic thinking. "It's horrible, how awful, it can't ever be fixed," and the like. Be kind and shift your thoughts. Tell yourself you kept your temper, or arrived on time, for example, and move on.

Please, avoid beating yourself up. Be compassionate to yourself. Be playful and keep it light. Refer to the earlier chapter on reworking your inner thoughts and voices.

Is This a Problem or a Habit?

Some problems are easily solved, while others are expensive or time-consuming. In either case, there's a straightforward path towards a solution. You fix your car after an accident or you clean up after a storm, right? Life continues unharmed. But if you frequently forget to fill your gas tank or snarl at loved ones and apologize again and again, where are the roots of these problems?

What sets you off? Start the **Reflect** part of the PARDA Process by determining if this is a situation you can fix immediately, or a habit you need to change. What are the roots? What information do you need to solve this issue? The Tools for

ACTion chapter reviews several strategies for problem-solving to get you started. Let your mind wander. Recall past incidents. What memories arise? What thoughts cross your mind? Write down the most trivial thoughts and ideas. Never brush them away by saying "they're stupid" or "too simple."

Regardless of the method, by addressing repetitive, upsetting thoughts sooner than later, it's easier to nip them in the bud and keep an emotional equilibrium.

Write It Down

The process of writing helps you identify patterns and triggers that get you wound up. Say you get stuck while writing about a topic, but later, a thought strikes you. A song on the radio triggers an idea. Write it down along with the date. When you **Reflect** on what you've written, identify what works and what doesn't. Keep your PARDA Process journal handy to track progress and make changes. Another advantage of writing is capturing ideas and insights.

Ideas are more slippery than olive oil. Sure, you'll always generate more of them, but a nagging sense lingers: You let something good get away from you. Next time write it down. A few words on the back of an envelope is enough if you have a file folder or box to drop it into for later exploration. In fact, make a note on your calendar when you intend to return to your written thoughts. You do intend to return to them, don't you?

"Write down the thoughts of the moment. Those that come unsought for are commonly the most valuable." – Francis Bacon

Your brain loves to solve problems, so use this trait to your advantage. You honor those insights by writing them down and acting on them. An internal part is rewarded when you do this consistently. While I've complained about having a brain that runs 24/7, I do appreciate all the solutions and ideas that arrive if I let them.

Writing Dumps and Rants

Because I'm writing anything from a few lines to several paragraphs five or six days a week in my journal, I'm pretty current on what bothers me. I keep telling people that you can run through the PARDA Process mentally once you get the hang of it but writing things down as brief notes increases understanding exponentially without taking hours of your time. These brief writings leave me feeling focused and calm. The notebooks are my "ten-dollar therapist" and I buy them on sale before school starts.

It's one thing to write stuff out and feel better. Your emotions range from irritated to grumpy or a bit sad. I use my writing to sort out conflicting ideas or problem-solve. Other times, I'm so furious I could spit nails. Those are the times I say things I bitterly regret later.

I struggle to sort out my angry thoughts. This is when I use longer writing sessions to explore my thoughts and gain distance. They only take 25 or 30 minutes but cut through the emotional storm. Everything, and I do mean everything, is dumped out. If the material is nasty or threatening, I shred those journal pages. No one gets to see my rants. While I usually save my writing, this category is the exception.

For many people, writing dumps convey to your body and the primitive parts of your emotional brain an event or situation is over. You've finished; you're free. Ripping up pages feels good.

When people write regularly, they become more comfortable with expressing raw emotions and anger. Their journal becomes the place to describe what they would like to do to a hateful neighbor or coworker. They often ask me whether or not to keep this material. No one needs to read this stuff. This is for you alone, which is another reason to prevent others from finding upsetting material. The pages are meant to help you detach from strong emotions that befuddle your thinking.

Toss these pages in the shredder. Some folks tell me they have a place where they safely burn their notes. Crumpled newspaper burns easily, but notebook or typing paper does not (voice of experience here). Feeding sheets piecemeal into the flames is time-consuming and possibly dangerous.

Here's an event that had simmered in my mind from years ago. I deleted the expletives, but everything else remains as I wrote it. While I normally do this by hand, I typed these words quickly, just as if they were written instead of typed. First, the back story.

Randy was a tech in charge of the mainframe system at a job I'd had years ago. He also monitored the telecommunications hardware and software. Since he had access to almost everything electronic within the company, no one wanted to get on his bad side, knowing the harm he could cause.

One day, I was helping a female coworker with her word-processing software and templates. Neither one of us could get the software to work properly, and we had to call Randy. He and another tech made snide comments about the incompetence of women in the department. By the end of the day, I was seething and did the following writing dump. Feel free to insert your own four-letter words:

I can't believe that jerk gloated over my screw-up trying to help someone with his document. Nance you're stupid lit me show you how to do it write as they exchange those man to man greins over female cluelessnesss. Where the heck does he think he gets off acting like a jerk over a mistake heavenforbid I do the samething back. I enjoyed the time he wasn't able to help someone and had to ask for help I was SOOOO nice and polite. But I didn't rubhis face inhis dumb mistake I mean he said he knows how to findstuff in the office yeah right.

I ranted and raved and wrote out all the nasty things I couldn't say to Randy in person. You get the gist. To further complicate matters, he was someone suspected of damaging employee software, making reports disappear, and more. People were afraid of him for good reason.

When I finished writing, I felt wiped out. I drank some water, puttered around the house, and put away the dishes. While I didn't reread what I wrote, the action of writing allowed me to come to a deeper understanding when I addressed my thoughts about the situation later.

First, I admitted I enjoyed retaliating by being scrupulously polite and giving Randy assistance when he asked for help. I didn't remind him what a jerk he had been, and I felt so self-righteous. I had to own that I was being as much of a jerk as Randy, just being subtler about it. But people aren't stupid. Randy knew I was extracting payback, and he hated me for it.

Second, this was a low-level feud that had been going on for months with me and others in the office. Randy delighted in aggravating people by exerting control over their devices. How much did I want to become involved and would it make a difference? I doubted it.

Third, I realized Randy could cause serious personal and professional damage. I had little or no recourse to resolve the situation. Some people were lucky enough to find employment elsewhere, but I didn't feel I could make a move at the time. Many continued to fear Randy and what he could do to their computers. Judging from their whispered conversations, nuggets of truth lay in their fears.

"Fill your paper with the breathings of your heart." – William Wordsworth

Finally, while I'm a Christian, I had to admit those nasty words were in my heart. To my shame, the rant revealed how much anger I felt and that I needed to ask God's forgiveness.

I'd like to say this issue was resolved quickly. It wasn't. After I had reflected on my thoughts and written them down, I had to create strategies. My first choice was to engage with Randy as little as possible. When we did, I worked at remaining neutral and matter of fact. Occasionally, I would ask a question about his evening classes.

One day, Randy told me he didn't understand why I didn't come to him for help with my computer and devices at home. Everybody else in the department did. This had bothered him, and I had no idea. While Randy exaggerated the number of people at work who asked for his help, he was right. I did avoid asking for help, although I knew he had excellent computer skills unrelated to his current job.

Taken aback, I blurted out that I already had a long-time relationship with another computer tech whom I turned to first with any problems. That was the truth. He could understand customer loyalty, couldn't he? The second part (which I didn't say) was I prefer to keep home and work relationships separate.

Randy and I never became buds, and our rift got to the point of his ignoring me whenever possible. Unless it was necessary, he'd ask others when he had questions. To my relief, he moved on months later, and I haven't seen him in years. I hope he found a place where he could use his skills productively.

Writing about my upset and rage allowed me to step back and make more reasoned choices. I put strategies in place, knowing the situation wouldn't change any time soon. Writing turned out to be a safe place to vent, along with kvetching to close friends outside the office. The writing and venting enabled me to make wiser choices and kept me from saying and doing things I'd regret later.

Not everything can be fixed. We do our best within a painful situation. By using the PARDA Process, we identify what we can change and move on from there. It does feel frightening to **Pause** and **Acknowledge**, let alone **Reflect**. We're afraid of the emotions and memories because we fear they'll be too painful to face. Or, if they can't be readily solved, we're afraid we'll be unable to cope with the long-term effects.

Using the PARDA Process resolves those nagging, everyday thoughts and events we deem trivial and shove aside. By being *with* the event—letting emotions arise and then ebb—healing often happens quickly, and we stop brooding.

Writing about all of this shortens the time we spend wallowing in painful experiences that sucks out our personal energy. **Reflect** allows us to separate the emotions from the events.

What is the Blessing in This Situation?

In addition to reflecting on what went right, look for the blessing in a situation. At the least, choose to learn from mistakes.

Child abuse is a terrible, horrible thing. Yet women have told me that once they began to work through their own abuse experience, they could see it gave them greater compassion for others—a blessing. I have seen survivors break years of familial abuse extending back generations by healing their own wounds.

Now, I'm not suggesting you grit your teeth and proclaim, "Oh, isn't this wonderful" in the middle of your challenges. A pastor once said, "Romans 8:28 isn't worth a pitcher of warm spit when you're going through a tragedy. But afterwards, you see how God worked in and through the situation." Hebrews 12:11 says, "For the moment all discipline seems painful rather than pleasant, but later it yields the peaceful fruit of righteousness to those who have been trained by it." (ESV)

I suggest challenging yourself to look back and see the blessings in past tragedies. Going through a life-threatening illness, for example, reveals the mundane parts of living from a whole new perspective.

Explore Your Gratitude

Sources everywhere extol the virtues of writing down what we're grateful for. We read, "Write down three things every day you're thankful about." "Keep a gratitude journal to help reduce stress and be more productive." This advice sounds helpful, but if it creates one more source of pressure, forget it. Studies confirm writing once or at most twice each week is enough.

Acknowledging with specificity what makes you grateful sharpens your awareness about what's going right.

"Learn to be thankful for what you already have, while you pursue all that you want." - Jim Rohn

Pausing throughout the day to breathe and allow spontaneous feelings of thankfulness and relief is beneficial. During the most troubled times, take a moment to extract a tiny smidgeon of joy.

When you **Reflect** on what makes you feel grateful, write a few phrases. I didn't realize until I wrote it down how organizing and straightening is soothing once I start. Walking through a local nature sanctuary is both relaxing and enjoyable. If I hadn't written down these observations, I would have forgotten I have many ways to cheer myself up instead of struggling.

By being specific about what lifted your heart, you intensify it. I'm reminded I need more simple experiences (not things) in my life to bring me joy. While I'm grateful for my laptop and cell phone, they don't make me "happy" per se. In fact, there are days when checking my email is a distasteful chore until I read a message from a loved one.

Actions that trigger sensations of gratitude are enjoyable and satisfying. The Great Recession taught us that staying home and being with loved ones was a source of pleasure. The monetary constraints increased our appreciation of what we already have. Writing down our feelings of gratitude helps us recall joyful moments.

Chapter 7

Decide

How do you make decisions? Do you throw options at the wall and see what sticks? Do you go online and see what others have done? Or do you sit down in a quiet place with your notebook and mull things over?

I've said it before and I'll say it again: We're not trained how to think and make decisions.

Most of us spend more hours planning a vacation than examining our expenditures or deciding about a job.

We all have different decision-making styles. What are the issues involved with making decisions? What will distract us or make us think more clearly? Is making time to think and make decisions all that important?

During the past several decades, scientists, psychologists and others have discovered clues to thinking and making decisions. Their discoveries, combined with what I've learned from the business world, has changed my views about thinking and planning.

Ponder, Think, Plan

What does it mean to think? Can we slow down the thoughts in our heads? Along with **Pause**, I like the word "Ponder." It means to turn something over in your mind. Contemplate. Review. Think through. How often do we take time to explore what we're thinking about? I love getting stuff done and moving on to the next thing. Unfortunately, in my haste to decide, I've made many mistakes along the way. It's incredibly tempting to consult the internet, talk to friends, and then go with the flow.

"Thinking: The talking of the soul with itself" – Plato

In so doing, I realized I was giving away my power to make create my own life, one that's right for me, not someone else. Once a decision is in place, *then* I'll run it past friends and loved ones. Ask for their input. Search the internet, all *after* I've taken a little time to think for myself. I may, or may not, accept people's ideas. It also means my choices might be unpopular. Do I trust myself enough to stand my ground, after I've thought something through?

"Executive function" is a popular phrase that describes abstract thinking, attention, and motivation, among other things. In concrete terms, it is the ability to figure out what needs to be done, analyze the steps and carry out the task until you're done. Many of us either didn't learn these skills as children or think it will be too difficult and time-consuming to even try.

Raymundo's Story

Raymundo was one of my clients in grad school. Stocky and barrel-chested with a head of thick black hair, he struggled to maintain his grades. He had a strong "B" going into mid-terms, but his scores on quizzes had dropped. The mid-term exam would count for thirty-five percent of his grade.

I left an email asking him to meet with me during office hours. We chatted about the hot weather and his girlfriend. Then I got down to business.

"Ray, what's going on with your quiz scores? You were doing well and now they've dropped. You know you need a 'B' average or you'll lose your scholarship." I waited. Ray started to talk, then stopped.

"Professor Larson, it's so hard to study all the time." I nodded in agreement.

The words tumbled out. Chaz, his buddy down the hall, decided he wanted to go out for a beer (or two or three) and banged on Ray's door. Ray had a choice: He knew he needed to study to get a decent grade on the exam, but he was fed up with hitting the books and was ready for a break.

I stopped him. "What went through your mind when you wanted to head out?" I knew there was a moment when Ray could have made a better choice, but would he see it?

Ray sat in silence, then spoke slowly. His slight accent deepened. "I wanted to go out. I was tired. But I also wanted to do well on the quizzes and mid-term."

"**Pause** right there." Ray cocked his head. "Just take a couple of moments to breathe and tell me more."

"I like going out. I hate grad school." He stopped, mortified about saying it in front of a professor.

"Ray, this is the place to let it out, four-letter words and all. This is what I tell people to do on paper. The trick is to dump it out without judging yourself like you did just now."

He bit his lip and looked at me. "I'm afraid I'm going to flunk out and let my family down. I'll have to find work landscaping like my dad and brothers instead of getting my MBA." He shared the love he felt for his parents and the pressure he felt being the first generation to go to college, let alone graduate school.

When I saw his shoulders sag and heard him sigh, I knew Ray had finished. Then I explained he had to **Acknowledge** without judgment the swirl of emotions, conflicting desires, and pressure he had pushed down inside. That's what he had just done. All he could do was summarize the thoughts and feelings of frustration and fear.

"So now what? All these feelings, what difference do they make? I don't like this soft stuff. *Madre Dios*, I don't want to talk like this."

"**Reflect** on what you just told me," I replied. "I'm hearing you tell me you want to stay in school." He nodded. "You're under a lot of pressure from your family and your own standards. You don't have to stay in school, since your dad would be glad to have you in the business."

"*Si, si*, yes. I want to be in the business, but doing the books, not cutting bushes. I want to make it bigger and better, hire more people." As Ray grew more excited, he lapsed into sporadic Spanish and gestured with hands calloused from outdoor work.

"What do you really want to do in terms of your degree?" Given his grades were starting to slide, I knew he couldn't waste any time.

"I want to finish school, Professor Larson, but I need time to relax. I can't keep looking at numbers all night and write Dr. Wilson's case studies." I had heard about Wilson's notorious case studies with their hard-to-find online sources and minimal information for students. His goal was to replicate what they would experience working in consulting firms.

We talked further and Ray **Decided** to take several steps. He needed to meet with Dr. Wilson and arrange for a writing tutor. His problem was writing, not numbers. He was doing well in his accounting classes, because he'd been keeping the books for his dad's landscaping business.

Ray didn't know if he wanted to switch his major to accounting, especially because it meant taking an extra semester. But he admitted he preferred working with numbers instead of the writing and research required for his MBA. He **Decided** to meet with someone in the accounting department and explore the possibility of changing. Then he could keep business as his minor.

We continued, exploring strategies for dealing with his buddy Chaz. When he wanted to go out, Ray decided he would go if he had been studying earlier in the evening. This also reduced his habit of procrastinating until 9:00 or 10:00 p.m. Going out later became a reward. And Ray was right; he couldn't keep studying without a break.

What was the first small step he would **Act** upon? It was reaching out to the writing center for tutoring.

"When will you call or walk over?"

"The center is open this afternoon, so I'll stop in on the way back to the dorm," he told me.

"No, tell me the time you will walk into their offices." Ray was too polite and respectful to give me an eye roll, but I knew what he was thinking.

"Okay, okay. It's two-thirty now; I will walk in at three o'clock."

Ray did graduate a semester later than he would have because he switched to accounting. And Chaz's interruptions became a non-issue for Ray after he joined two accounting groups with participants who were disciplined about studying.

Decisions Are Draining

My mom used to say, "I tell myself I'll do it tomorrow and tomorrow never comes." Getting rid of clutter is tiring because of all the decisions involved. Keep or toss? If I keep something, where will I put it? If it's a discard, do I give it to charity or toss into the trash?

"A wise man makes his own decisions, an ignorant man follows the public opinion." - Grantland Rice

Psychologists claim we start the morning with a certain amount of energy for making decisions. As we keep making choices through the day, we get tired. This fatigue explains why we buy a blouse or a multipurpose wrench on the 2:00 a.m. shopping shows we would have ignored earlier. Here's an experiment that sheds light on this.

In an upscale grocery store, psychologists Sheena Iyengar and Mark Lepper displayed twenty-four different flavors of jam. To everyone's surprise, they found that consumers were ten times more likely to purchase jam on display when the number of jams available was reduced from twenty-four to six. Less choice, more sales. These results have been replicated with numerous other products and services. When people have too many choices, they don't want to put extra effort into deciding. Too much choice drains our energy.[17]

Taking mindless, tiny steps reduces decision drain. You could download the application for a job now and fill it out later. You could clear off half of the kitchen table and challenge yourself to keep it clear for seven days. At the end, assess how it went and whether to continue.

First as a therapist and now as a librarian, I continued to be floored how often I sit down with someone who has a question such as, "How do I plan my kid's college graduation, then three weeks later get him set up in his new digs to start a job 500 miles away?" They come in for a book on party planning, and within seconds I hear the entire story. When there's time, I give them some paper and pen and suggest they summarize the situations on two separate pages: Graduation Party. Moving. Then I ask them to jot down their worries. Finally, we put the worries in some sort of order and possible steps to solve them both.

At the end of the process, which usually takes less than ten minutes, the person stares at me. "I've never had someone break it down like this." Once they see this overwhelming problem chunked into parts, they get moving, and momentum takes over. Then they can use the internet to find party supplies and consult with friends on an experienced mover.

What follows are several issues around making decisions that I've experienced myself, or when I've helped others. There's no one, perfect way to make decisions, nor are there any guarantees. Flexibility and being receptive to new ideas are the keys.

Are You Deciding or Justifying?

Our minds are sneaky. Some decisions are easy, but when we do ask others for advice, will we listen, let alone follow through on their suggestions? It's one thing for Andrea to call her friend Rosa and go back and forth about signing up for the art class she's always wanted. They talk about the time involved and how much fun it is to buy art supplies. Conversations between friends are entertaining in themselves. Whether or not Andrea signs up for the class isn't a big deal.

At work, Bill tells Jim he's going out with the new programmer in the department. Jim brings up several concerns, but Bill brushes them off. "Hey, it's just dinner with a coworker." Jim wonders if there will be any blowback if their manager finds out. "Nah, we're meeting at a restaurant by my condo." "What about Sue, your girlfriend?" Bill replies, "Sue's been working late and doesn't mind."

Do you see my point? Bill has made up his mind to ask this girl out, while Jim is hoisting red flags. Is Bill trying to get Jim to tell him it's okay, "go for it"? If your close friend or loved one is raising concerns about your course of action, are you man or woman enough to sit in the discomfort of their questions? Are they seeing through your rationalizations?

We used to joke in grad school about the Bible verse that says a prophet is without honor in his own country. It referred to "advice" (nagging) we receive from family, friends, and loved ones. They mostly have our best interests at heart, telling us what we already know but don't want to hear. We're more inclined to listen to advice from professionals such as doctors, lawyers, and accountants because we pay them a fee for their services.

Of course, we already know certain things because our parents told us to be polite, eat properly, and get enough sleep and exercise. These are all obvious, but most of us (me included) don't do them as much as we should. We must challenge ourselves to make commitments and slant the odds of success in our favor.

One of the benefits of being honest about acknowledging and reflecting is making thoughtful choices rather than justifications. Will you make the wrong decision from time to time? Of course, but I hope you'll minimize the potential for disaster.

Insight Doesn't Generate Change

Prisons house many inmates who know they have a problem with drugs or alcohol. They say they recognize they can't resist the next big score to impress a girlfriend, but nothing changes.

Insight alone doesn't lead to action. While so-called "talk therapy" is helpful for exploring emotions, afterwards I say to myself and clients, "Now what?" This is where the PARDA Process balances both cognition and action.

From what you've read so far, I hope you know I'm in favor of counseling. When you're in emotional pain so deep you can't see straight, a professional shows the way forward. Medication helps if prescribed by a qualified healthcare provider who monitors its effects.

Willpower Doesn't Work

I repeat this point yet again because we think we're "bad" if we can't change or do something on our own strength. We forget that advertisers play to our desires. Restaurants set up their menu, the lighting and a host of other parameters to prey on our hunger. No wonder we succumb. We berate ourselves needlessly, since psychologists and scientists are finding we have a finite amount of willpower. (Think about figuring out what to wear in the morning or filling the gas tank before or after work.) All these "little" decisions drain our willpower reservoir before we ever reach the office. By mid-afternoon, we find we're either not making decisions or we take the path of least resistance.

This shows why decluttering our desk (or our lives) is so draining. All those little decisions zap us. It's a powerful reason for taking those tiny, minute steps (detailed in Chapter 9).

Decision-making Style

Research shows our temperament drives our decision-making style. Author and psychologist Heidi Grant Halvorson, Ph.D., found people fall into two categories: Preventers and Promoters.[18] Preventers like to figure out how to make everything go right. They regard small mistakes as devastating, and they want to hang on to what they've already got. It's hard for them to believe (or trust) things work out for the best. Being alert and vigilant, they use prevention strategies to avoid the worst.

By comparison, Promoters explore innovative ways of doing things. They make mistakes and then toss out the results and try something else. They are optimistic and creative. Unlike Preventers, they focus on the gains and positive outcomes of a project.

According to Halvorson, those in the first group want safety and security. They don't play to win but to avoid losing. Their work is thorough and accurate. But, they aren't known for their growth and innovation. This is a prevention focus.

The second group responds to optimism and praise. They take chances and seize opportunities; however, they are more likely to make mistakes and not think things through. This is a promotion focus.

Both viewpoints, taken to an extreme, are annoying. I've worked with Promoters who are highly creative, and I'm floored when I hear their ideas. But I've also had to clean up after their mistakes. They move on to the next shiny big thing and lose interest in earlier projects.

I've also met Preventers who are compulsive about everything being perfect. I bite my tongue instead of saying, "Enough already." It's hard for them to risk criticism and they're reluctant to put their work on the line. How many people have you known who plan an event then make dozens of minor changes, making everyone crazy in the process?

Do you need to change your decision-making style? No. Instead, find the sweet spot that works for you and your team to get the job done.

Clinical psychologist and Harvard professor Sherry Turkle described students who spend needless time crafting the "perfect" email rather than risk a mistake sending it.[19] I've seen coworkers who can't stop revising memos, graphics, computer programs, and everything else. I struggle to stop writing and revising so I can ship my "baby" out into the world. Believe me, I understand why people want their efforts to be perfect.

You already know which category you fall into. Either you plan and figure out all the steps ahead of time, or you plunge ahead, saying, "I'll make it up as I go along—no problem." Neither style is better or worse than the other, but it will make a difference in outcomes depending on the strategy.

Most of us are dominated by one style or the other. It takes discipline to stretch our focus into the other mindset. Preventers need to trust they've prepared enough and move on. By contrast, Promoters must step back and recheck their efforts, ensuring they've covered all the bases. That's why I hope the pilots on any flights I'm on have done the preflight checklist more than once. Mid-flight is not the place for surprises. By contrast, I appreciate marketers focused on action who generate multiple promotions at the same time for different companies.

Head or Heart Decisions?

Everyone thinks we must select one or the other: logic versus feelings. For most decisions, it doesn't matter in the grand scheme of things which choice is best. Others tell me they're right-brained and can't do the logical stuff, Plus, it seems so, well, cold. Scientists have discovered that the right brain/left brain split is a myth. When they hooked up subjects to devices that measure brain activity, they discovered the blood flow was strong on both sides of the brain, regardless if the experiment was designed to measure logical versus creative thinking.

"If your head tells you one thing, and your heart another, before you do anything, you should first decide whether you have a better head or a better heart." - Marilyn vos Savant

Yes, people do seem to do better with logic, while others think more in terms of pictures and relationships. In either case, learning to flex between the two provides the best results.

Did some decisions turn out to be terrible, like marrying someone who later cleaned out your bank account and ran off with someone else? Of course.

Mike Dooley, founder of Notes from the Universe and The Universe Talks (www.tut.com), once wrote, "Aim with your heart, steer with your mind, and know that it always works." To be honest, I've wondered about how it all works out, but Mike had the right idea to use both your heart and your mind to guide decisions.

When we ask God for wisdom and expect He will grant us clear guidance for the next step (but not always the result we seek), He will answer. (James 1:5).

We want things to go our way, but what if God has something better in mind? Whenever we set goals and outcomes, we must allow God to lead us in another direction if He desires. More than once, I wanted a certain job or go out with a certain guy, but God slammed the doors tight. Later, I could look back and feel grateful I accepted God's will instead of my own.

There are times you look back and see your mistakes as if in Technicolor. "I should have heeded the warning signs. I should have done something different." Stop. Ask instead, "What did I learn from the experience? Did I ignore red flags raised by friends and family?

Using the PARDA Process lets us work with our heads and our hearts. We need both for making decisions.

It Doesn't Have to be Perfect

Barry Schwartz, author of *The Paradox of Choice: Why More is Less*,[20] claims that people are either "Satisficers" or "Maximizers." The former group has certain parameters or guidelines regarding their choices. Once they find something that meets those criteria, they're done. They're satisfied. And they don't agonize after making decisions.

Maximizers, on the other hand, want to make the optimal decision. When they find whatever meets their needs, it's not enough—they keep looking. They expend considerable time and energy to ensure they made the right choice. Unfortunately, they're worried about making the *best* choice. Satisficers, according to Schwartz, are generally happier and less anxious than Maximizers.

Most people are a mixture of both Satisficer and Maximizer. I scour sales racks in clothing stores and I adore used bookstores. If I find something, I'm happy. If not, that's okay, too. But when it comes to choosing a new health care provider or dentist, I have exacting standards. Then I keep looking "just in case." When it comes to health care decisions, I'm a Maximizer.

Choose when it's important to **Decide** according to your exacting standards, and let the rest go.

Balance Perfection and Failure

It's easy to obsess about getting out the perfect report or having the laundry impeccably sorted and folded. I suspect it's because we enjoy the immediate sense of fulfillment when a job is completed. This is true when it didn't take much time or brainpower. We get something out of the way that doesn't have much importance, and it's enjoyable. The brain doesn't care about the level of difficulty, just the endorphin rush of satisfaction.

Some business gurus advocate "fail fast, fail often." This bothers me because we put our mediocre efforts out too quickly. We're allowing the world to shape our efforts. The novels of Jane Austen remain in print more than a hundred years after her death. There is a Jane Austen Society, and her books are the basis of successful movies. Did you know she wrote six novels, and two were published after her death (*Persuasion* and *Northanger Abbey*)?

If Austen were alive today, she would be pressured to crank out a new book annually. During her lifetime, she didn't have the tyranny of social media and bestseller lists, and she could take her time. Similarly, when we value ourselves and what we offer the world, we will take time to do it right.

We can't be Maximizers with every choice, but I question whether we decide too quickly on serious issues. I can't choose for you what to maximize on or when to be satisfied with a "good" versus "great" choice. I do believe, however, we need to remain true to our core values and what's important to us, whether others agree with our decisions or not.

Conditions and Constraints

When I couldn't do what I wanted, or something wasn't possible, my dad would say to me, "These are the conditions that prevail." I knew that statement marked the end of the discussion. I hated those words with a passion. As I've gotten older, however, I realize he was right. Some realities won't change.

One of my employers used to say, "You can have the results fast, cheap, or in-depth. Pick two." A nearby coworker used to mumble, "If you're lucky, you'll get one of them." That meant our clients couldn't have it all and had to set priorities.

"The more constraints one imposes, the more one frees one's self. And the arbitrariness of the constraint serves only to obtain precision of execution." - Igor Stravinsky

The challenge is to remain objective and not let emotions distort our thinking when we encounter immovable obstacles. How we label them is the initial challenge, which is why it's critical to take time to **Acknowledge** and **Reflect**.

You're a single parent who lost your job, and you have three children under the age of ten to support. Waves of panic flood your body. Where will you find another job? What about food, clothing, childcare? There are no easy answers. What if you receive a job offer elsewhere? Your children love their school and your sister provides back-up child care. Is it wise to move?

Another constraint could be physical limitations. You find it difficult to lift heavy boxes or walk several hours. These constraints may never change. Vocational rehabilitation counselors with disabled clients must examine their clients' capabilities within their parameters. Because of your situation, maybe you need a desk job rather than one that requires you to work in confined spaces. The challenge is to acknowledge your limitations without becoming angry, bitter, or frustrated to the point that you can't come up with alternatives.

Depending on your personality and disability, it can take years to accept difficult parameters without bitterness, let alone come to peace with them. It's common to underestimate the depth of sadness, loss, or other emotions attached to limitations. It's okay to let those old thoughts arise. In fact, I suggest doing the PARDA Process multiple times without the need for action. Clear your emotional decks repeatedly until you come to a decision.

My Uncle George always said time was more valuable than money. Up to a point, money and possessions are replaceable, but once time passes, it's gone forever. Our elders tell us they wish they had spent more time with their spouses and children. A medical diagnosis forces us to realign our lives in a hurry. I've been unemployed or doing part-time work. That meant I had time for personal projects but not the funds. Now I'm fortunate to have a full-time job, but it cuts into what I want to do. How will I use my time?

Energy is another challenge. I have time, money, or both, but do I have the energy to take on more activities? I'd love to be out more with friends, but I've learned if I push myself too hard, I get sick.

Entrepreneurs use constraints to devise new ways of doing business because they don't have the wherewithal for tried-and-true approaches. Understood, constraints enable them to focus their choices. There are several ways of looking at limits, but no one can avoid them.

Setting and Keeping Boundaries

We impose our own constraints, called "boundaries." Saying "No, I can't chair the decorating committee this year because I have other commitments" is not being bad. We let people make us feel guilty when we set our commitments above theirs. If allowed, people will give us responsibilities that don't belong to us.

I didn't mind sharing my notes with a fellow classmate who was absent because she had the flu. After she asked me three or four times, though, I stopped helping her. My resentment over being used collided with my wanting to be a "nice" person. It's hard to watch hurt looks sent our way when we hear the classic, "If you loved/liked me, you would _____."

Setting boundaries and saying "no" keeps people from taking advantage of our good will. And saying "no" is not being negative. A pervasive negative attitude douses icy water on everyone else's ideas. "Negativity thinkers" describe everything as wrong, impossible, or worse. There's no exploration of possibility.

On a happier note, when we say "yes," people realize we're honoring them by giving them our time, energy, and skills. Instead of being agreeable to be liked, we choose to say "yes" because we want to bless someone or give with no strings attached. Resentment is less if we know when to say "yes" or "no" as part of keeping our boundaries with others.

Sunk Costs

The term "sunk costs" refers to something you've put money into and will never be able to recoup. Originally a business term, it's also a way of looking at the cost of a relationship, a job, or other situation and deciding if the potential profit is worth the cost. Otherwise, cut your losses and move on.

When I realized I wasn't using my degree for a career in vocational rehabilitation, I took a deep breath and walked away. Working for a large organization didn't fit who and what I am. I thought everything was over.

"But...but you spent all that money on a degree," people said to me. Yes, I did. Still, through years, I've used the skills I gained from those courses and work experiences to help people find jobs, identify their strengths, and do what vocational rehabilitation counselors do. The difference? I use these skills in a setting that's different from a conventional practice.

How do you discern when to keep going or close it down? Ask yourself:

- If someone came to me with this issue, would I tell that person to stop? If yes, then tell yourself the same.
- Is the time and energy expended worth the result?
- Will things improve if I keep throwing money at it?
- With respect to relationships, how long have I stayed with no change in behavior despite repeated apologies and tough conversations?
- Deep down inside, do I want to change but fear I'll look stupid?

Sunk costs help you acknowledge what happened and start anew. The expensive car and payments eat your paycheck, so you sell it at a loss and buy an older sedan with smaller payments. You've invested years in your education, but there are no more jobs in your field. You'll never recoup what you spent in tuition.

Affordable Loss

Entrepreneurs and small business owners take risks to grow their business. This is the idea behind "affordable loss," which asks questions such as: "How much can I afford to lose? How do I take realistic steps without wiping myself out?"

A guy I knew in high school purchased a seat on one of the exchanges instead of going to college, much to the dismay of his parents. I used to run into him on the train going home from work, and he looked the epitome of a prosperous banker. Neil was doing well financially, despite not going to college. I asked him how he did it.

"I'm still living at home, so my expenses are low. From my paycheck I put aside money in my emergency fund that I can't touch. Then there's the rent I pay my folks and gas for the car. You know, the usual stuff." His next category, however, caught my interest.

"I set aside money that would have gone toward tuition. This is what I use for risky bets. It's for learning what they don't teach in school." I waited, hoping for stock tips. He went into a lengthy description of stock terms that went over my head. But his next words took my breath away.

"Yeah, I lost over twenty thousand dollars the previous week." I stared. This would have been almost a year's salary for me at the time.

"Neil, are you out of your mind?"

He shrugged. "Like I said, it's money that I could afford to lose. It was an expensive lesson, but I have my savings and still cover my expenses."

Looking back today, his explanation made perfect sense. Neil gambled with what he could afford to lose and was willing to take risks to gain experience. Years later, I learned he married and moved to Palo Alto, California. Knowing Neil and his philosophy, I'm sure he could well afford it.

Navigating Uncertainty

Actuaries, loan officers and insurance underwriters have the skills and tools to quantify risk. Uncertainty, not knowing, is a far bigger challenge than risk. How do we make correct decisions? We estimate the costs as best we can in terms of time, costs, and a host of other factors. Unfortunately, no matter how hard we try, we can't guarantee the outcome. No one can.

When it all falls apart, that's the time to **Pause, Reflect,** and go through the steps. Dig deeper despite any discomfort you feel. To reinforce what you learned from the whole mess, write notes in your PARDA Process journal. Always take time to **Reflect** on the logic of your choices. When I started my first full-time jobs, logic dictated that, years ago, I should have stayed at a job in the city and kept my current salary. The amount was far more than an appealing position closer to home.

In another instance, I "should" have gone elsewhere to a position requiring me to drive more than two hours each day because of potential for advancement and training. In both cases, my heart wasn't in it. Do I honor my heart or my head? In both cases, I couldn't figure out a solution no matter how much I thought. Ignoring logic, I went with my heart. Who knows what the best decision should have been, but I was at peace with my choice.

If you're leaning on the facts in a situation and the outcome is unclear, *feel* your way to a solution like I did. According to neurologist and author Antonio Damasio, if there are multiple rational alternatives, the heart will guide the mind.

"Exploring the unknown requires tolerating uncertainty." – Brian Greene

When faced with challenging decision, I suggest taking an extra-long **Pause**. Seldom do you have to decide right this second. Seek God's wisdom. Do your research. Talk to others. Look at your decision from different angles. Let's say you want to attend college in another city. It has a great program in your major. You love their reputation for having loads of hot babes or stud muffins walking around campus. But a little voice in your head reminds you if you attend this school, you'll have more than $80,000 in student-loan debt. Gulp. You're tempted to ignore the facts and go with your heart. Is that a wise choice here?

I don't know what the answer is for your situation. I do think, though, if you seek God's will and go through the PARDA Process, you will find clarity. Let's say that after considerable prayer, thinking, and writing, you decide it's worth going into debt because there's long-term high demand for graduates in your field. If so, then research the best loan options and scholarships.

Suppose you have two job options. The first is close to home and provides a good salary. The second pays somewhat less and you must drive longer than if you took the first one. But the second job stirs your heart and gives you a pleasant flutter in your stomach. Which do you choose?

The phrases "Follow your bliss" and "Do what you love, the money will follow" are questionable in today's job market. Most of us don't have the luxury of those options. But is it an either/or decision? Not usually.

Ask yourself a few questions. How old are you? If you're able, take the job that gives you a flutter in your heart for a year or two. If you find out after nine months or a year it wasn't a good fit, ask why: Was it the people? Less than satisfying work? Ask, "What did I learn from the experience? How will those experiences affect my future decisions?" Your answers become valuable feedback.

Questions in the Middle of the Night

Let's say you've been offered a promotion. Everyone around you tells you what a big step up it would be for your future. Your spouse is thrilled about the pay increase. Yet you feel uneasy and wake up during the night. What are the responsibilities of the new job? Do you want to work an additional ten or fifteen hours each week? Or (if it's a transfer) do you want to uproot everyone to a strange city with new schools for the kids? Your mind spins as you lie awake at 3:00 a.m.

It's time to go through the PARDA Process. Get up, turn on a light, and grab paper and pen. Before you do anything else, **Pause**. Breathe three or four breaths. Become calm, and in faith, ask God for His wisdom. (James 1:5)

Acknowledge your emotions in the moment. Scared? Pressured? Curious about the future? Write. Let the words flow and overlook any spelling and grammar mistakes, as shown here:

Do I want to do this? Everyone tells me what a great opportunity, but I don't think I want all the hassle for what amounts to small increase in pay, all title no money, my dad used to say why take this on sure wish I could do something different this isn't what

I signed on for. Melanie thinks it's a great idea should I try for this, no, yes

Keep writing for at least ten minutes. Set a timer to beep but keep on writing without stopping sooner. When you finish at the sound of your timer, take a couple of breaths. Don't look at what you wrote quite yet.

Reflect on how you're feeling. Writing out all your mixed emotions, including the unpleasant ones, will help you find clarity and detachment. What do you experience in your body? Where do your muscles feel tight? Both feel and think about what you just wrote. You realize you're not enthusiastic about this promotion at all. At the same time, you know your spouse believes in you, and your manager thinks you're qualified. Are you responding out of fear of the future, or do you dislike the responsibilities involved? There is no right or wrong answer—only what you, not your spouse or manager, is feeling.

Decide on specific steps and write down a few ideas or alternatives. Do you need to gather more information about the responsibilities of the new position? If a transfer and a new house are involved, might you talk to others who have transferred into your department from other divisions? Will the initial amount of overtime increase or decrease as you understand your responsibilities? Don't make your decision until you gather the information you need.

Act on just one small step. For example, you could clarify with your manager what your specific responsibilities will be. Or, you could identify a date and a time to meet with a recent transferee away from the office. What additional steps could you take after meeting with someone?

While you gather information, do another PARDA Process. Lather, rinse, repeat until you're ready to stop. In this way, you're putting your emotions, thoughts, and actions into balance.

God Didn't Answer

I do ask God for wisdom for my decisions, and I already hear people saying, "But I did ask, and I didn't get an answer." Personally, I'd like Him to send me a text with detailed instructions, but so far that hasn't happened. Human nature being what it is, would I obey if He did?

In general, does God want us to work at changing habits and making reasoned choices? Should we just sit and wait for instructions? At what point do we act, then look to Him for help when we've reached our human limits?

I suspect these questions are behind the push-pull of faith versus works, thinking we make all the effort on our own without God's help. If we believe in justification by faith alone, are we saying our own efforts are wrong? No. When I drive my car, I ask for God's protection over me and my passengers—but I also buckle my seatbelt and use my turn signals. I ask God to provide for my needs, but Paul reminds us that those who don't work, don't get to eat. (I Thessalonians 3:10) We're told "faith without works is dead." (James 2:26)

People quote Ephesians 2:8-9 (ESV), which reads, "For by grace you have been saved through faith. And this is not your own doing; it is the gift of God, not a result of works, so that no one may boast." Verse 10, however, is usually ignored: "For we are his workmanship, created in Christ Jesus *for good works, which God prepared beforehand,* that we should walk in them." (ESV, italics added) God intends us to do "good works," even as we are saved through faith. Our works are not the means of salvation.

God enjoins us to commit our ways to Him, but we also need to think and plan, as these and many other Bible verses indicate:

- "Commit your work to the Lord, and your plans will be established." Proverbs 16:3 (ESV)
- "The plans of the diligent lead surely to abundance, but everyone who is hasty comes only to poverty." Proverbs 21:5 (ESV)

- "Prepare your work outside and make it ready for yourself in the field; afterwards, then, build your house." Proverbs 24:27 (NASB)

We can't say, "Oh, the Lord will work it out," or "the Lord will provide," and then do nothing. I experience an ongoing tension between what God does and what I need to do, then step out in faith.

I recommend making sure your choices and decisions follow biblical principles. Most people who complain they don't know God's will for their lives don't seem to have a rudimentary understanding of God's most basic values, found in the Ten Commandments as a basic starting point. If you are Buddhist, Muslim, Jewish, or adhere to another set of beliefs, it doesn't matter. These religions all have a code of conduct, and while the principles seem simple, they certainly aren't trivial.

Let's make it simple: "Do unto others as you would have them do unto you." Islam: "None of you [truly] believes until he wishes for his brother what he wishes for himself." Buddhist: "Hurt not others in ways that you yourself would find hurtful." For a lengthy list of these principles, see the Religious Tolerance site at http://www.religioustolerance.org/.

Chapter 8

Act

Once you have decided on a solution or you want to make a change in your habits, what's your next step? Do you have moral parameters? Do you know what hinders you? The temptation (and I've done it) is to create a mega-list—elaborate, detailed to-do lists that are impossible to achieve. Instead of taking one small step, I run full-tilt and lose steam. Then I beat myself up for not finishing.

"Well done is better than well said." – Benjamin Franklin

Our brain finds change difficult and scary. It says, "Don't rock the boat. Wait! Stop!" The solution is to find tiny, miniscule actions that don't rouse a brain that's hard-wired to resist change. That acronym KISS—Keep It Simple, Sweetheart reminds us to stay simple. What small, ridiculously tiny step propels you toward a goal? The temptation is to say it's too simple, or that small actions won't make a difference. Not true. Small steps, done consistently, yield big results. This chapter features a mix of strategies to help you implement whatever decisions you make. Progress, not perfection.

Physicists tell us an object in motion stays in motion, and objects at rest stay at rest until acted upon. Neuroscientists know this: Brain cells that fire together, wire together. This tells us the value of habits to get us started and maintain momentum.

The sections that follow spell out general principles regarding your decisions and subsequent actions. God may reveal *what* to do, but you still need to carry it out.

Note: People have argued with me about every portion of the PARDA Process. They don't have time to **Pause** or it's too painful (or terrifying) to **Acknowledge** their emotions without judgment, let alone **Reflect** on what happened. Trying to **Decide** what to do next is difficult. Relying on small steps to **Act** takes too long and seems stupid.

My response? You've tried everything else including crash diets and pulling all-nighters. You've struggled to incorporate more relaxation in your life on the advice of your doctor. Nothing has worked, so please humor me and try making it easy on yourself.

When you've made your decision to move forward, do a reality check. What is your desired outcome? Is it realistic? If there's considerable risk involved, how willing are you to accept the consequences, both good and bad?

If you still feel scared, are you at peace with yourself, sensing this is the right thing to do? Then take the plunge, knowing you've done your best with the knowledge you have right now.

Act with Integrity

We pretty much know we're not supposed to steal or kill someone, right? I suspect, however, most of us slip with regard to trivial things. We "borrow" twenty dollars from a friend and forget to repay it. Somebody takes the "leftover" desserts in the cafeteria home several times a week. Someone else leaves five minutes early or takes "a few minutes extra" for lunch.

The Bible says he who is faithful in little will be faithful in much. (Luke 16:10) How much do you rationalize your actions? Do you have a vague awareness of discomfort about something you did years ago?

One definition of character is "what you do when nobody is watching." If you knew God/your mom/your kid was watching, would you behave differently? Today, everyone is watching. When you don't expect it, what you said or did goes viral on the internet (as celebrities learn to their dismay). Once forgotten, minor infractions now lurk online forever and are found in nanoseconds.

Acting with integrity when no one is watching builds character. Think of it as a micromove, a pattern you strengthen with time. Hopefully, it will keep you from engaging in actions you'll later regret.

Give Yourself Permission

Give yourself permission to experiment. Talk back to the voices who put you down. For inspiration, read the biographies of people who pulled themselves out of terrible situations. Learn about Oprah Winfrey's beginnings and Abraham Lincoln's repeated business and political mistakes. Or Steve Jobs. While creating Apple, he overcame numerous problems. These role models succeeded despite tremendous obstacles, so look to them for inspiration.

Here's a way to simplify your reading. No matter how fascinating the individual, I don't have the stamina or energy to read an 800-page book. Instead, I head over to the Young Adult section of the library. Librarians who specialize in materials for teens offer a goldmine of recommendations. It's a lot easier to read fifty or a hundred pages to become inspired than eight hundred of them.

When we lived in small towns or close-knit city neighborhoods, everyone knew our business. We bought into perceptions such as "She'll never amount to much, she came from the bad part of town." "You're going to college? Seriously? You've got to be kidding." "He's a truck driver, so what does he know?" Envision those snarky comments accompanied by rolling eyes.

Self-limiting comments include "The economy will never get better" or "they say things will get worse" or "you have to know somebody to get ahead." Trying to block out these phrases to keep yourself in a better frame of mind is hard. Depending on the speaker, you don't want to alienate someone or get into an argument.

Take small steps toward your goals and talk back to the internal voices raising doubts in your mind. Get out of your rut and take a chance.

You Choose Where to Improve

Once something becomes routine, do you want (or need) to improve? We cultivate specific habits and go on autopilot for brushing our teeth or making breakfast. Musicians, athletes, and artists as well professionals such as scientists and engineers create daily practices. How? By focusing on one specific problem and how to solve it.

Suppose you're struggling to master your golf swing and you hire a pro to guide you. The pro watches you and grabs your shoulders. "Here's one of your problems," she says. "Your right shoulder lifts at the wrong point in your swing." During the practice sessions, she works on your shoulder position. She tells you to practice the shoulder move ten times for short periods during the week. The new swing seems unnatural, but you practice despite your doubts. The change becomes part of your skill set, and you realize the golf ball now flies down the fairway in the correct direction instead of veering off.

Work on One Issue at a Time

It's up to you to **Decide** where you want to improve your life and dedicate the necessary practices and **Actions** to do so. No one tells you where change needs to occur; you choose for yourself. A plan, combined with choices in steps, removes the emotional charge keeping you from starting a task. *"I made the plan, I'm making the choices, and I retain a sense of control."*

Along with deciding where you want to improve, focus on one issue and be willing to dedicate weeks and months if needed. Say this is the year you decide to work on keeping the house clean—something you've struggled with for ages. You're doing it because this is important to *you* (not your mother-in-law, nor your spouse). Therefore, be specific and define what a "clean house" means for you. A "clean house" is a vague, global resolution.

Exactly how will you make it cleaner? Fewer dirty dishes in the sink? Papers filed or discarded regularly? Laundry done twice a week?

New Year's resolutions fail because they contain no plan on how to achieve specific results. Therefore:

- Keep steps small—ridiculously tiny.
- Work on one issue at a time.
- Go slowly and take a month (or longer) to make it a habit.
- Choose actions you control, not someone else.
- Tweak details as needed.

Your PARDA Process belongs to you. Give yourself choices. The decision to **Decide** on a course of **Action** is yours. Yes, you need to address how your steps will affect others, but this is your decision, as are the consequences.

No Perfect Time or Action

"I'll be happy when I get a promotion." "I'll start exercising after Thanksgiving." "I'm waiting for the perfect job and the salary to match."

Stop waiting for the perfect relationship, job, or a certain income. By waiting "until," we postpone happiness. "I'll be happy when I finish school." "When I find the perfect guy/gal, I'll enjoy life." "My life will be great when I get the promotion and pay off all my debts." The more scientists studied happiness, the more they found we don't know what will make us happy. We forget to appreciate what we already have. When we play the "wait until" game, we discover too late life has passed us by. Worse, what we thought we wanted left us feeling either empty or dissatisfied.

"The undertaking of a new action brings new strength" - Richard L. Evans

One way to deal with things you don't want to do is postpone the dreaded task. Do it tomorrow or next week. Today, you're tired or busy or the weather is bad. But this will be true a month or six months for different reasons. Life never slows down—you will always be busy.

Take It Slow and Savor

Taking time instead of rushing lets you focus and find enjoyment in the process. When I clear a stack of dirty dishes from the table, I recall the meal everyone just finished. I savor hot, soapy water on my hands. I'm grateful for a home with running water and food to feed myself and others. This is a far cry from racing through scraping dirty pans and rushing off toward something else. By focusing on my **Actions**, I have a sense of connection to my loved ones and the satisfaction of completing a simple task.

Brains can be retrained to enjoy the moment instead of feeling rushed—if you're willing to work at it. Focus on the enjoyment of small steps, accumulating day by day like beautiful pearls on a string. Make sure you give yourself the rewards you promised. Create new habits and all the changes will build on one another.

Do the Hard Stuff First

A huge boost to your efforts is getting the hard activities done and out of your way. Savvy business owners have found that by doing their difficult challenges in the morning, they get more done and experience a sense of accomplishment. Furthermore, they build momentum by these challenges.

"If it's your job to eat a frog, it's best to do it first thing in the morning. And if it's your job to eat two frogs, it's best to eat the biggest one first." – Mark Twain

This concept isn't for business people alone—it applies to everyone. Certain household jobs are my equivalent of eating frogs. Taking the bathroom rugs to the laundromat and scrubbing the floors before I put them back are my frogs.

Identify the date, time, and place to begin a large project and what you intend to accomplish. If you're planning a large move, decide when to sit at your desk and make a list of all the items you have on your mind. No order, just spill it out. Then when you look at the list, you'll find yourself arranging things by action or grouping projects.

For example, if you're moving in October and it's March, sort seasonal decorations and pack them now. The tools you inherited from your dad are boxed up and put in storage. Pick the date, time, and place for another small step and move on. The days before your move will be crammed with activities, but you've already strategized your activities and decided on the most efficient ways to accomplish them.

Identify Possible Outcomes

Ask yourself, "If I knew the solution I seek, what would it look like?" If the solution you come up with seems outlandish, suspend judgment for a few moments. Be playful. Know that a great solution could pop in your mind later that never would have occurred to you earlier. This is different from visualizing a goal without taking the steps to achieve it.

When you think about deciding, determine what you want as an outcome. How will you know when you've achieved your goal? What will be different? What benchmarks will you use for complex goals? Must the outcome be perfect, or will you be realistic and accept a different result?

Suppose your company wants to hire a new employee in the marketing department. The Human Resources department received dozens of résumés. You or a group takes a first pass and eliminate more than half of them. Upon further examination, nine or ten candidates meet the specific parameters for the job. Unfortunately, none of them meet all the key criteria. You and your team plan to interview the five best candidates, a time-consuming process. You all agree the second candidate is a real keeper. Do you hold the three remaining interviews? Or once you've reached your benchmarks, do you stop interviewing?

How long will you keep looking, rearranging, cleaning, rewriting, or whatever? When does the amount of improvement become minimal—or make things worse? What benchmarks indicate you're done? Your decisions won't always be perfect, but if you've done your homework, talked to trusted individuals, and done as much as you could, take a deep breath and implement your choice.

W.H. Murray, author of the book "The Scottish Himalayan Expedition writes:

"...that the moment one definitely commits oneself, then providence moves too.

All sorts of things occur to help one that would not otherwise have occurred. A whole stream of events issues from the decision, raising in one's favour all manner of unforseen incidents and meetings and material assistance which no man would have dreamed would come his way."

Chapter 9

ACTion Tools

Making new habits and sustaining change is hard work. Like everyone else, I long for shortcuts and eagerly search for ways to make life simpler. Since I'm a reference librarian and self-help seeker, my antenna is always scanning for ideas. When you experiment with different tools, you learn what suits your personality.

I sure don't have all the answers, but in the following pages I include several strategies I've used to keep me motivated. Numerous websites, articles, and books list more helpful ideas, and at the end of this book, I've included a short Resources section to get you started.

Accept that our brains thrive on challenges and questions. When we combine a questioning mind with a playful spirit, answers show up in unexpected places. We hear a chance comment from a stranger or stumble across a web page that has the answer while we're searching for something else.

The more we relax and make it a game, the faster the results. These days, I've stopped wondering why this works and enjoy the experience.

Use the following suggestions to move forward with small steps. Sit down with your PARDA journal and do the steps **Pause, Acknowledge, Reflect** without skipping to **Decide** and **Act**. Writing out your thoughts gets your brain moving and will generate additional ideas. Make a list of ideas and steps, but don't worry about making it perfect, just get something down in writing. Make a messy list, put it aside, and come back to it a few days later. You'll find your brain keeps generating more suggestions. Do write them down so you don't forget. When you return to your list, strategies will become apparent.

These ideas are in no particular order, so start with what looks appealing. Give it a good shot and adapt them to your situation.

How Do You Get It Done?

When you sigh about not being able to keep the house clean or follow up on your emails, **Pause** for a moment. Examine the issue. What is disturbing about the emails? Relax, breathe, and step back. **Acknowledge** there's a problem: Why are emails such a challenge? You hate going through email, and it piles up. You're missing important memos. It takes too long to sort through them. Or the topic is too painful. Like Scarlett in *Gone with the Wind*, there's always tomorrow—until there isn't—and you're in a crisis.

Write it all down as a dump in your PARDA Process journal. When you **Reflect** on an issue, recall any areas in your life when you felt on top of certain tasks. Do your bills stack up and go unpaid, or do you process them when they arrive? How is that different from the email? What systems do you have in place to get unpleasant stuff done?

"Routine, in an intelligent man, is a sign of ambition." - W.H. Auden

What distasteful chores do you complete regardless of your emotions? What threat would force you to keep caught up? The threat of trashing your credit keeps you current on the bills, so what would be comparable to keeping you current on your email?

If you can't take multiple days off, what about other rewards, like fresh flowers or a latte? Whether you realize it or not, you have a routine or process in place to pay the bills or get to work on time, including during a snowstorm.

Take a few moments to think about how you finish something you dislike. What are the rewards? Where is the willpower? What are the painful consequences?

As you **Reflect** on an icky task, identify possible connections. The dreaded report reminds you of homework in grammar school, and you realize you have the same sense of dread. What's the source? Do you hate writing? Feel rushed? When you realize why you struggle with the report, you start to separate past emotions from current reality. While the reports seem like busy work, they need to be written. Is there a way to streamline the process? Start sooner? Develop a template?

Take a few minutes to explore and create micromoves that enable you to get those reports done with less stress. Recall a time when the report flowed, and to your surprise, you turned it in on time. What was different? What went right? Give yourself time to let memories like these come to the surface.

Decide you will have a solution, although you don't see it yet. You and everybody else hate these reporting requirements. What kind of information do you need? Are statistics and activities tracked by several individuals? Is it a collaborative effort bottlenecked by a couple of people who procrastinate? Who writes these reports quickly and without angst? What is their secret and ask them to show you their process for getting it done. People are usually happy to give advice.

Pace Yourself

Regardless of the tools you create, pace yourself. Stop pushing. I can't stress this enough. Pushing yourself to exhaustion probably got you stuck in the first place. Although I've suggested pausing and savoring, pacing yourself conserves your physical and emotional energy.

We hate to leave a job undone, it's part of the human psyche. At the same time, this is where pacing yourself becomes a challenge. Leave some energy in reserve. Going full-out, even with proper planning, leaves you exhausted. One benefit of holding back is to fuel your desire to keep going and finish.

This is a fine line to walk. On the one hand, if you're close to finishing a project, it makes sense to push through, wrap things up, and savor the satisfaction. On the other, if you promised yourself you'd stop before exhaustion sets in, you've violated an internal boundary. When you ignore self-imposed promises and boundaries, you'll be less willing to take on new activities or projects—and rightfully so. Your body and soul are exhausted, and any sense of satisfaction is drowned out.

Finally, stopping before you're ready helps you look forward to the next day. This hooks the part that hates to leave things undone. Use this itch for completion to stay motivated.

Daily and Weekly Routines

Our lives are routine. Get up. Brush our teeth. Grab a bite to eat. Go to school or work. We long for excitement and a break in our routine. Paradoxically, routines anchor us. If we had to rethink every time how to brush our teeth or tie our shoes, our lives would bog down.

When we have a routine, we stop arguing with ourselves. If we automatically hang up our clothes when we get home, it becomes a habit that pays off in less mess. Life is simpler.

"Routine is a ground to stand on, a wall to retreat to; we cannot draw on our boots without bracing ourselves against it." - Henry David Thoreau

Micromoves, as I wrote earlier, help us figure out what actions work for us personally. We can create routes and systems that might be "just good enough" instead of fretting about perfection. Routines free up emotional and mental energy.

Our emotional, physical, and mental buckets are full first thing in the morning (this is true for night owls as well). As the day progresses, we make choices. Do we select eggs for breakfast or plain yogurt as a healthier choice? Do email right away or start the audit? How do we resolve conflict among employees?

The day ends, and we wonder why we're tired. Heading home, we don't want to cook so we stop at the deli for a salad and sandwich. "Not perfect, but at least the salad is healthy," we think. The more we automate our lives, the more we free up energy to go deeper with what's important to us before we're too drained to think straight. Mindfulness has its place, but routines lighten our mental bucket.

Use Triggers to Your Advantage

Addiction counselors warn their clients to stay away from places and situations that trigger their urge to drink or use drugs. Their clients find themselves meeting an old friend and together they start drinking or drugging all over again. The addiction trigger is automatic...until they learn to rewire their response to it. Why not use this part of our brains for good?

Triggers are one of my favorite ways to get things done without stressing out. In her book *The Creative Habit*,[21] dancer Twyla Tharp claims creativity is a habit. Every day, she goes to the gym or works on her dancing. She starts by getting out of bed, throwing on her clothes, and grabbing a cab. The trigger of getting into the cab gets her going. She doesn't argue with herself; she just gets dressed and enters the cab.

When I come home from work, I change clothes, have dinner, and flop into my favorite reading chair. Changing clothes and seeing the chair triggers me to say, "I'm done for the day, as in done, done, done." Except I'm not.

I want to work on my creative projects and not collapse. I'm experimenting with triggers to get me to sit down and work longer. One trigger is confining my work to a certain desk. When I'm tired, sitting there tells me I'm ready to work. Turning on my computer and putting on my "magic writing ring" shifts me into writing and revision mode. To reduce distractions, I turn off email and the internet.

I used to work at a reception desk shared by multiple users. Out of courtesy, we tried to keep clutter and personal items to a minimum, but some were more successful than others. When Brenda showed up for her shift, she fascinated everyone by filing papers and putting folders in the cabinet. She ruthlessly sorted the catchall receipts basket. While her hands moved, she made conversation and asked how we were doing. Her fingers flew as she continued to straighten up the desk. Indeed, whenever she saw a messy area in the office, she organized it. Seeing clutter and disorganization triggered her to clean. It was amazing.

Identify your own triggers and then use them to instill new habits. When I get out of bed in the morning, I make it. I also rinse my breakfast dishes and stack them in the sink until evening. These habits started when I was a child during a time we put our house on the market. We never knew when the real estate agent would call with a potential buyer in tow, so everything had to be immaculate.

I had to hang up my clothes in the morning, put toys away, and dust. When the phone rang, Mom put our dirty dishes on a baking sheet and shoved them into the oven. We stashed unwashed clothes under the bed. She moved the knickknacks to temporary storage. A phone call from the estate agent became a trigger for a cleaning binge. I'm compulsive about making my bed and hanging up clothes to this day.

If-then Strategies

Suppose you have trouble starting something, let alone finishing it. Dozens of studies have shown if we create strategies to deal with obstacles before they arise, we avoid arguing with ourselves. *If* this happens, *then* I will do that. *If* I eat five chocolate chip cookies, *then* I will get up fifteen minutes earlier for two mornings and do more exercises. *If* I finish writing this chapter early, *then* I'll email my friend Dale.

Why does this strategy work? My sense is because you have a plan in place and your brain doesn't need to make decisions. This works for both pleasant and unpleasant situations. In my Psychology 101 class we learned about Premack's Principle, also known as Grandmother's Rule. Grandma tells her grandchildren,

"*When* you finish your dinner, *then* you can have dessert." "*When* you finish cleaning your room, *then* you may go out and play."

Give yourself a boost by writing down your "if-then" planning This one helps me become real and stay on track: "*If* I'm tempted to play a game on the computer, *then* I will write five hundred words first."

Becky's Story

Becky, a new insurance trainee, told me she knew she had to do a certain number of cold calls each week. The company didn't care when they took place, just that she documented whom she called and when. She said she hated them because of the endless number of rejections before one prospect responded. Becky knew calling was a numbers game, but it bothered her.

"I know I can do this. I keep telling myself they're rejecting my product, not me. But I hate cold calls, so I bunch them on Friday and rush to get them done and leave by 4:30. They hang over my head all week."

Becky **Paused** and let her thoughts and emotions swirl around the act of cold calling. She sighed. "I know it's part of the training process since I haven't built a client base of referrals. Still, I hate the tightness in my chest, and I'm scared I'll be written up for not following through."

I asked Becky if she liked the company's product. Why did she sell insurance? Her face lit up. "I saw my best friend lose her dad from a heart attack. She was ten years old and he was in his late thirties. He had some life insurance, but her mom had to go back to work. My folks used to have Paula over after school and lots of times she stayed for dinner." Becky connected the impact of unpleasant events in people's lives, and the importance of having insurance.

Then she **Acknowledged** the positive emotions and reasons for insurance along with her distaste for cold calling. "Which feeling is stronger?" I asked. Becky **Reflected** on Paula's experiences, and the effect on her own parents. Seeing what happened to Paula made Becky's parents increase their insurance coverage and put more into savings.

With the first three steps of **Pause**, **Acknowledge,** and **Reflect** completed, Becky **Decided** she needed a strategy to get her calls out of the way sooner. We explored several ideas. Becky chose to make one telephone call when the clock said 10:00 a.m. and another at 11:30 before lunch. She put an "X" on her calendar for each one. (X's and checklists). To minimize distractions, she turned off her email notifications and checked in three times a day.

I asked Becky when she would **Act**. "Well, this is Wednesday. I'll start my plan on Monday."

"What's stopping you from doing it right now," I asked. "Sure, most of us start resolutions and plans on Monday, but why wait?"

When Becky reconnected her emotional purpose for selling insurance, it became easier to connect with prospective customers. When she became discouraged, she thought about Paula. When a customer purchased coverage, Becky made a note to track her successes. Within a couple of weeks, she was completing most of her calls well before Friday.

Small steps make course corrections easy. Trust the PARDA Process by giving yourself time to change the steps and tools.

Use Checklists Creatively

When you were a kid, do you recall seeing rows of gold stars or stickers on a chart? Earning a certain number of stars meant you received a reward.

This works for adults, too. When you have a calendar on the wall and place a red "X" when you complete a micromove, it becomes harder to break an extended chain of red marks. This little action has huge cumulative effects. Besides the calendar, keep track of successful micromoves in your PARDA Process journal. Enjoy your successes and reward yourself.

Creating visible checklists keeps you on task and reminds you about periodic rewards. When you make micromoves, the Xes on checklists keep you from floundering and giving up. Don't scratch off your tasks. Instead, use a colored highlighter. On my to-do list, I cross it off in pink when I finish a chore. What a kick to see most of the items covered in glowing pink. I see what I've done rather than fret that I missed something. Somehow, if I scratch something off the checklist, it's as though I didn't do it in the first place, and I've lost a sense of accomplishment.

"The checklist is one of the most high powered productivity tool ever discovered." - Brian Tracy

Earlier, I mentioned using time and place notations—that is, make a note when you find your best "flow" or "energy" states. It's time to reread your notes. Is your best energy related to location? Time of day? What's different compared to the days you feel bogged down?

Making notes about this taught me how I underestimate the amount of time I need for tasks. It also revealed that my energy levels for mental tasks is highest in the morning. Creative types say they get their best work done late at night when the rest of us sleep. Other people rev up as late afternoon approaches.

Give yourself permission for self-praise—your version of gold stars—when you finish your chores. Little kids love to tell everyone about their gold-star accomplishments, and adults are no different.

Accountability Partners

People ask me if accountability groups and/or rewards promote finishing goals. It depends.

Being part of a team or having workout buddies forces you to show up and do the work because you don't want to let people down. When a friend sends an email saying he finished revising a difficult section of software, I'm thrilled, and I shoot off words of praise. I've acknowledged his accomplishment, and he does the same for me. Friends treat you with kindness and support you when you're down. It's comforting to have friends who will listen to your difficulties, even if they don't have answers. It's like the old Irish saying, "Joys shared with friends are doubled and sorrows are cut in half."

Trustworthy partners and friends point out our blind spots and weaknesses. I find it easy to feel defensive when someone criticizes me for being too analytical or slow. Depending on the project or goal, being accountable is either a blessing or a curse.

Because I prefer to work by myself, the thought of team meetings is appalling. But I don't work in isolation. Being able to email or call my friends to crow about how well I balanced the checkbook is my reward for completing a distasteful job, and their teasing about my ineptitude with numbers makes me laugh.

Still, be careful whom you ask to be your accountability partner. If you ask your spouse or significant other, will you become angry when he or she asks you if you exercised or paid your bills as planned? I'd rather keep my husband as my husband, not as my parent.

Does your friend praise you, rather than say, "Gee, I'm surprised you didn't finish the project over the weekend?" Anyone you select for an accountability partner must be supportive, so spell out the check-in parameters. Is it a text? A scheduled breakfast or lunch? Phone calls? On your part, what will you do or complete?

Incentives and Disincentives

Disincentives are another "stick" or threat. If I don't finish an important project, then I'll write a hefty check to a cause I detest. That's a disincentive. For example, if you're a staunch conservative, you'd write a check to the opposite party. Do you love to eat meat and feel proud of it? Then send money to an animal rights group. Believe me, this kind of accountability step hurts, and you'll do anything to avoid the pain.

A more palatable version I've heard from sales people is giving their administrative assistant twenty-five dollars on

Monday morning. For each completed cold call, the admin keeps five dollars. By the end of the week, the goal is for the assistant to keep the entire amount. Sales people feel guilty about giving their assistant less than twenty-five dollars, so they stay late to honor their commitment. Landing one or two new clients each month from those efforts more than pays for the expense.

A variation is to agree to give your accountability partner fifty or a hundred dollars if you *don't* complete benchmarks as promised. Depending on your income, decide how much will hurt. It should be hefty enough to sting when you fail. After paying up once or twice, most of us will stay on task.

Of course, the strategy works both ways: Your partner pays *you* if he or she fails to meet the stated goal. For me, the biggest challenge is taking the money and saying thank you. You can't tell your buddy it isn't necessary to pay it back or you'd splurge on a dinner together because it doesn't feel right otherwise. Nope, enjoy it. If you can't enjoy using the reward for yourself, give it to charity.

If you reward yourself, play fair. When I complete writing two thousand words, I allow myself to go to the bookstore with a clear conscience later in the day. I know I can pretty much go whenever I please, but there's disappointment in my heart if I "play" before I finish my writing goal.

I've also declared in writing that when I complete a certain number of words for the entire first draft, I treat myself to a one-hour massage. When I finish my revisions, then I treat myself to a special breakfast.

I suggest being realistic when you plan rewards. Sure, I'd love to book a trip to San Francisco or New York once this manuscript gets published, but that's pricy. Enjoying time at a luxury spa is more realistic, plus it means I've gotten away from my computer. The bonus? I gain peace of mind without worrying I overspent.

Make It a Game

Scrimping to save money or scrambling to change a spending habit seems like enduring unrelenting pain. I've learned to mix up strategies to make the process more palatable.

Here are games friends and I have used to monitor our spending, get a job, and still have fun. I've also used games to make housework more interesting. Experiment and create games of your own.

Live like a Grad Student—Graduate students are notorious for living on noodles doused in ketchup from fast food joints to stretch their food budget. Don't get that desperate. Instead, cultivate the habit of finding ways to make everything stretch besides food. How low do I go? What purchases could I postpone? Should I buy or rent? Is the item available used instead of new? With websites such as Craigslist, eBay, RetailMeNot, and others, it's easier than ever to find bargains in good condition. Savor the virtue of living frugally for short periods.

A variation is to live close to the bone for four weeks. That means no meals out and no purchases except for emergencies or medicines. Eat leftovers and clean out cabinets and your freezer. Track what you save and then transfer that amount to your savings account or use it to pare down debt.

Joy of the Score—Living like a grad student naturally leads to celebrating bargains. I've seen friends and coworkers snatch up amazing finds in thrift shops, consignment stores, and antique malls. It's a kick to see them show off their designer clothes or an old dresser refinished to look new.

Let's Pretend—The best time to find a job is when you don't need one. If you're terrified of job interviews, do several while you're employed. When you feel scared in the interview, put on a bold face and carry on. This kind of pretending works at parties, networking events, and other places that push your discomfort levels through the roof. I like to pretend I'm my friend Leslie who acts at ease in groups of strangers. Who knows? You might gain an unexpected interview or make a new contact in the process of pretending.

Planned Splurges—Set aside five dollars regularly and find ways to treat yourself. Fresh flowers? Jewelry on sale? Premium ice cream? Put unused funds aside and combine them with the next five dollars. Once a week or so, plan a splurge. I have fun with this game. For years, I met a friend for breakfast at a café where $4.25 with tip covered my meal. The fifty or sixty cents carried over to the following week. Now, because we meet evenings, we head over to a local restaurant for dinner instead of breakfast.

Those little splurges avert feelings of deprivation that lead us astray, especially when we tighten our belts for awhile. Then we pretend we're grad students again until it's replenished. Knowing "it's not forever" makes the process tolerable, if not easier.

Wants List—When I stroll through a store or mall, should I buy something if it's on sale? If the thought persists, I write it on my Wants List to dissipate the intensity. Why this works, I have no idea, but I've kept my Wants List notebook active for years.

For me, doing this game revealed how many of my wants were based on the moment. Some items have remained on my list for ages, like returning to Toronto for a visit or taking an extended road trip. Other wants were practical, such as a new stove and refrigerator. Writing them down got me comparing brands, searching for sales, and putting extra money aside. To this day, I enjoy the appliances we purchased with the added satisfaction of paying cash and putting a small amount on credit.

Ignore the Sales Alerts—Take glee in seeing how fast you clean out your email box by deleting sales alerts. Combine this with *Living Like a Grad Student* and enjoy staying within your budget. When store clerks ask me for my email address and I give it, within hours I'm inundated with messages trumpeting "4-Hour Flash Sale." To make it worse, they send multiple alerts. For many of us, the word "Sale" creates an urgent sense of "I must have _____ right now." Resist temptation.

Anyone who works retail will tell you stores have sales about every six to eight weeks, depending on the product. Some items, such as school supplies, go on sale in mid-July. That's when I stock up on copier paper, pens, sticky notes, and the like for the rest of the year. Bedding goes on sale in January, new cars as early as August. According to my husband, stores regularly put frozen meals on sale. He stocks up and fills our freezer. Yep, I'm guilty. Some nights we don't cook from scratch. The Wants List helps me keep track of items and find them on sale.

For the most part, I ignore the sales alerts unless I'm already near the store and stop in. Some people set up an email account solely for sales alerts. This removes the temptation to buy something in the moment while tracking alerts if they're on the prowl for a bargain.

Housework Games—Cleaning the house or your home office is ripe for games. How many items can I pick up and put away from the living room in fifteen minutes? Will I finish cleaning the bathroom sinks before the rinse cycle starts on the washing machine? How many papers do I throw out to create a two-inch gap in my file drawer? What kinds of rewards—from reading the newest J. D. Robb mystery to going for a walk in the woods—can I give myself for my efforts?

WOOP It Up

No, "WOOP It Up" isn't a party, although you'll celebrate when it works. Psychologist Gabriele Oettingen, in her book *Rethinking Positive Thinking,*[22] asks her clients to identify a **W**ish, see a specific **O**utcome, envision the **O**bstacles, and make a **P**lan.

The first half of her book described her experiments with various groups of people who wanted to complete a goal. When Oettingen did the research, she learned that subjects who identified potential problems ahead of time and made specific plans to deal with them were far more successful in completing their goals than those who didn't.

"One who gains strength by overcoming obstacles possesses the only strength which can overcome adversity." - Albert Schweitzer

Researchers discovered that changes were carried over after finishing the study, as she reported in *Rethinking Positive Thinking.* On her website "WOOP my Life" (www.woopmylife.org), she leads the viewer into tailoring her process to their needs. It's easy enough to vow you're going to go to the gym. But what happens if it's too cold outside? Or you worked overtime the night before and got home late? What obstacles are in the way of your plan?

According to Oettingen, those who identify obstacles and create specific alternatives are more likely to achieve their goals. This means writing down your plans for inevitable obstacles. Incorporate your "if-then" strategies. "If it's bitterly cold, then I'll stay at home and use an exercise DVD for an hour." "If I'm overtired, then I'll work out for half the time and take a walk at lunch." These options reduce the anger and guilt you feel for not following your original plan, and lets you move forward.

Piotr's Story

Encouraging people to identify their challenges and solutions is fun.

Part of my job as a librarian is helping small business owners grow their companies, giving me opportunities for one-on-one sessions with patrons. Piotr owned a carpentry business passed down from his father, but many of his clients had aged and no longer needed custom-made furniture. He knew younger people were moving into affluent areas of the city and could be a rich source of new clients. He met with me to brainstorm how to find new customers.

"I need to market my business, but I know how to create good furniture, not advertising programs," he told me with a slight accent. "Where do I start?" I told him to **Pause**, then asked him to describe his current clients while comparing them to what he wanted in the future. "That's easy. Most of my old clients are from Poland and the Ukraine. They're older with more money, and they want a nice cabinet or custom storage unit for their home." His old clients lived in homes located in upscale, older suburbs.

His new ideal clients would be younger. Plus, they needed smaller pieces of furniture they could use in city apartments and condos. Piotr wanted to reach the growing number of young professionals moving into the city to be close to their work. The certainty in his voice told me he'd been studying his new customer base.

When we began to **Acknowledge** his comments, Piotr's emotions surged unexpectedly. He worried about taking his father's business in a new direction. His parents had returned to Poland, but still, he didn't want to let them down. He was excited about growing his business but felt scared, too. What if he failed? What would his parents say?

Piotr began to **Reflect** on his feelings and the steps he needed to take. Ideas spilled out quickly. He would gather testimonials from his clients. He would show additional photos of completed furniture on his website. "My head spins," he said. I listened to his plans then challenged him to identify obstacles—and how to work around them. Immediately, he said his lack of social media skills hindered him. He'd have to hire someone to update his website, then manage updates himself. "Good," I said.

What else could he do to reach young professionals? He said he didn't fit in with these hip, educated young people. "I am a tradesman; I don't have the schooling." As we continued to talk, though, Piotr described the carvings he did to unwind that he lovingly polished. Bingo. I challenged him to display the carvings in local galleries. "But," I continued, playing the devil's advocate, "what if the gallery owners reject you?" He shrugged. "Then I try another one. I think a local restaurant shows paintings. Who knows, maybe the owner will put my carvings on a shelf for sale."

By now we were cruising. He had an idea, and I playfully tried to talk him out of it. He would counter with specific steps to work around my objections. Soon he had more ideas than he knew what to do with written on his yellow notepad.

"Okay, Piotr. **Decide**. What's the next, easy step?" He decided to interview companies that designed social media for business owners. Wisely, he chose not to use friends. "Too messy. I keep business and friends separate." And once his website was up and running, he would ask his satisfied clients for testimonials and plug them in.

He told me his first **Act** would be to go for a beer to stop his head from spinning with all his latest ideas. When I looked at him, he grinned. "No, just kidding. I'll go online and look for web design specialists for half an hour when I get back to the shop. Too much to do, I have a shop to run, you know." His gorgeous blue eyes twinkled.

Piotr's vague goal to "grow his business" became focused because he created several strategies and identified the specific actions he needed to do.

A year later, I saw Piotr's carvings and a chest of drawers with a parquet wood top in an upscale gallery—with hefty prices to match. I hope he's doing well.

Chapter 10

Micromoves

Chapter 9 described tools and strategies to help you make changes. Ideally, you will modify them not only to suit your personality, but also devise small, structured steps. I keep stressing that small steps, consistently applied over time produces results. Called "micromoves," they're the secret weapon (in addition to writing dumps) for completing painful tasks and changing long-standing habits.

We already know how difficult it is to make decisions, let alone deal with change. Our brains are hard-wired to perceive change in terms of possible danger. Small moves allow for experimentation and course corrections without triggering fear.

The Practice of Continuous Improvement

A popular Japanese business concept is called *kaizen*. According to the Kaizen Institute (www.kaizen.com), it's "the practice of continuous improvement in which big results come from many small changes accumulated over time." It was based on the theories of Dr. W. Edwards Deming, an American business consultant who encouraged companies to self-analyze and critique themselves so as to continuously improve their companies. Desperate to rebuild after World War II, the Japanese adopted Deming's philosophy.[23] This was the beginning of *kaizen,* which means "improvement." It didn't include the concept of continuous self-improvement until later.

Here, I choose to extract *kaizen* from its business roots, while retaining the idea of making repeated slight changes for ongoing improvement in one's life. I call these minute changes "micromoves." They allow us to sneak under the radar of our ever-vigilant brain that resists change. The purpose is to treat ourselves with care and create permanent improvements over time. After you've done the acknowledgment and reflection steps, what will you do next? It doesn't have to be a major life shift. Think of the Japanese process called *kaizen* that encourages people to make continuous improvement in their lives by implementing minute changes.

My favorite example for small changes concerns exercise. Start slowly. While watching TV, you could do two lunges during one commercial break. After a week or less, you may find yourself doing three, four, or more of them during all the commercials. And because you're doing those lunges, you're not shoveling potato chips or ice cream into your mouth.

Keep finding other opportunities. At lunchtime, you go out for a walk instead of eating at your desk. Bit by bit, you make exercising part of your life. In this chapter, I'll use getting yourself to the gym as an example to explore micromoves.

Micromoves, as I define them, are the smallest steps we *consistently* perform to achieve our goals, regardless of personality and thinking style. Micromoves are small by design. They advance us bit by bit, with the operative word being "consistently." We focus on the immediate present until something is completed in that moment.

Micromoves engage us because they don't threaten our brain's need for the status quo. They allow us to nibble away at a problem without needing to resolve it all at once. Therefore, mistakes are smaller and carry fewer consequences. Why? Because it's easier to change any process in small increments.

"Big things have small beginnings." - Prometheus

No Skipping or Putting Off

Because micromoves are tiny, you must commit to performing whatever micromove you have created for your designated amount of time—no skipping or putting off. If you find yourself resisting, then decrease the size of the commitment. Once you have performed your micromove for the day (or a certain length of time), stop. Don't do anything more. If you find yourself wanting to do "just a little bit more," don't. Honor the commitment you have made to yourself to do that one small step and nothing else.

When you decide to increase your activity, that decision becomes another conscious commitment to doing a certain amount. You decide to commit to paying bills for ten minutes on Monday and Wednesday nights after dinner. Once you've done that, stop with a clear conscience, even if there's more to do.

The following week, you increase the time you commit from ten to twelve minutes. While it seems to take forever, you will catch up on the backlog of balancing your checks and examining your credit card slips. Without realizing it, you've become more careful about filing the receipts in a safe place until you reconcile them with your bank statement. The payoff comes when you catch an erroneous transaction. You prevented possible fraud in your account, thanks to your new watchfulness.

Nick and Amber's Story

Washing dishes seems trivial, but for Nick and Amber, the chore cast a pall over their time together. I saw them at the library when they were in grad school. Both felt fortunate to find jobs after graduation and they soon married.

During grad school, they subsisted on canned goods and frozen meals. Once they got jobs, they reveled in eating out. Like most of us, though, Nick and Amber realized they needed to reduce their spending by eating healthy meals at home instead of going out. One would cook and the other would wash the dishes. Neither of them wanted to do dishes, so they decided to rotate the cooking and cleaning.

Amber complained, saying, "Nick comes with these elaborate meals that take forever to prepare, and I'm left with a huge pile of dirty dishes to scrape and clean. With two of us, why use the dishwasher for one meal? Plus, the heavy pots need the burned pieces scraped off before we put them in the dishwasher."

"Amber, you enjoy the meals I cook. I'm trying to get us to eat healthy instead of slapping something together," was Nick's rejoinder. He told me they grilled chicken breasts, made salads, and prepared various vegetable dishes during the week. Because they both hated cooking and cleaning up after long hours at work, their dishes piled up on the weekends—along with feelings of resentment.

After hearing that jab about the dishes, I challenged them to make one miniscule change, a micromove. Instead of washing all the dishes, they could soak the pots and then, carefully and mindfully, wash *one* dish. Just one, no more. I told them to time how long it took to do that. Nick and Amber exchanged looks.

"You're suggesting we leave everything else in the sink?"

"Yeah, but on second thought, wash one dish before you head out on Saturday and another on Sunday morning. Then go about your day." My goal was to shift them out of their disagreement and alter their thinking and emotions around this problem. I was curious what would happen, or if they would follow my advice.

Several days later when they dropped off their books, they came over to the reference desk to talk.

"Do you know how hard it is to walk away with one dish washed?" Nick shook his head as he said it.

Amber chimed in. "We still had all those dishes to do on Sunday night because we both want a clean kitchen to start the week. But we timed it. It took me less than ten minutes to place everything in the dishwasher while Nick scrubbed the pots that had soaked for two days, also for ten minutes."

I felt like having a little fun, so I told Nick and Amber to wash *two* dishes on the following Saturday morning and one on Saturday night. Leave the rest.

That's when they stared at me.

"You're joking," said Amber. I kept a straight face.

"Give it a shot. What have you got to lose?" They both walked out shaking their heads.

The next time they showed up looking for more recipe books, they lingered. Sheepishly, they admitted they had rinsed off all the dishes and let them accumulate for a few days. Then they ran the dishwasher on Friday night. Sunday, they ran it again with the rest of the dishes used over the weekend.

These moves were trivial yet doing them forced them to shift their thinking. "It turned out doing dishes was a small thing," said Amber, "and we had been spazzing about it. Nick was the one who wanted to be the gourmet chef. But I convinced him it was okay for us to have fun and cut back on the fancy cooking."

What micromove would address a stubborn habit? Try it. Afterwards, identify what worked and what didn't.

Why Do Micromoves Work?

When people ask me why micromoves work, I include basic information about the brain in my explanation.

The amygdala is a small, almond-sized nodule deep within the older part of the brain, always alert for threats and. Micromoves are a way to move ahead at your comfort level. They sneak around your resistance or fear. Starting is the biggest challenge. Ask what stops you and examine your thoughts about it. "It's too hard." "I hate doing ____." What micromove will get you moving out of this stuckness?

Let's be honest. We've all made New Year's resolutions that don't even last until Valentine's Day or the goal/intention/change leaves us paralyzed. Let's use working out as an example. We whine, "But I don't *want* to get up to go to the gym." Write down your thoughts about working out.

With your thoughts written out, do you see any patterns? What are your specific obstacles? What easy steps get going instead of staying in bed? Will you meet a buddy you don't want to let down? Like Twyla Tharp, put your clothes by the door, and get ready on autopilot?

An initial micromove is getting out of bed and putting on your workout clothes but no further. You then change out of them without guilt. In fact, you don't leave the house. Give yourself permission to say "no" multiple times. One morning after getting in your workout togs, decide when you'll get in the car and drive to the gym. There, you'll do ten minutes on the treadmill (no more) and go home.

"Nancy, you're nuts. Ten lousy minutes?" Never mind—get in the car and stop arguing. Ignore the voices telling you to continue and go home. Be sure to do this for at least a week, and preferably two weeks. No fudging. Next try the treadmill for ten minutes, or five bicep curls, and go home. Resist the temptation to push harder. Since I am prone to overtraining, slowing down remains one of my hardest micromoves.

"It is to our own detriment that we underestimate the might of small and simple things." - Richelle E. Goodrich

If you continue to be kind to yourself, the result will be a solid habit. I can't stress this enough: *Make small moves.* The goal is to build habits tailored to your personality. When you commit to a micromove, it should be so small that you have no difficulty performing it for a certain length of time. There is one ironclad rule: you must commit to that miniscule move for however long you have decided.

Sweeping changes seem to work at first, but they leave people feeling exhausted. "Never again," you say, and you beat yourself up for not following through. Because your body dislikes sudden change, decide what you'll do to replace undesirable habits. Ensure new strategies avoid the same old binds.

Micromoves have enhanced my ability to monitor my efforts by experimenting with small steps and sequences. I can see if (or how) my life changes and modifications are easier. My parents used to say, "Something is better than nothing." Small moves done over time have a cumulative effect. We're conditioned to take big steps and miss our goals. We tell ourselves we can't think smaller, because we don't think it works. Our inner critic demeans consistent small efforts.

Micromove Ripples

Earlier, I wrote about making up the bed each morning as a child. Then I started hanging up my clothes as a habit instead of dumping them on the bed, so I didn't wrinkle the spread.

"Great things are done by a series of small things brought together." - Vincent Van Gogh

While I've noticed a trend back to the spring and fall cleaning ritual, it doesn't teach people how to stay on top of clutter before it becomes unmanageable. Living on my own in a small space, I noticed my dresser drawer was jammed, so I tossed a sweater or two. I had blouses in the closet I seldom wore so I got rid of them. Without realizing it, I started discarding stuff on the spot rather than waiting to do it all at once. It was easier to put stuff away, and a new habit was installed.

Because of their simplicity, micromoves create ongoing ripples while we develop new habits. Instead of struggling to fix everything at once, try one or (at most) two simple changes. Step back, evaluate, and select another micromove.

I'm still learning to use the PARDA Process skillfully. But now there's a way to offset my tendency toward grandiose plans. It has forced me to be more mindful of what I do and how I cram too much into one day. The hardest part is trusting that these micromoves will lead to big results. Experiment and learn what works for you.

Here's the payoff: If you're patient and trust the process, you will see an end in sight. Thanks to the ripple effect, you will find yourself easily making course corrections and creating new habits.

What Do Micromoves Look Like?

The possibilities for micromoves are endless and again, should be kept miniscule. Your goal is to create new habits while experimenting with small changes. Be prepared to realize that some changes, such as my disasters with fitness center memberships, won't work. Commitment to micromoves prevent me from stalling and making excuses. "I'm too tired." "It's too hard." My perennial excuse is "I don't feel like it." It's amazing how often I don't feel like doing something.

My friend Jess lost her mother after a short illness and had to clean out the house and do paperwork. She felt discouraged. One night, she called me and said, "I took fifteen minutes and sorted my bills. I haven't paid them yet, but they're sorted." A few days later, she said she spent fifteen minutes putting away the holiday decorations. She takes fifteen minutes at a time to work on the estate. She spent more than fifteen minutes on these activities when she had the time. Breaking tasks into fifteen-minute micromoves reduced her guilt and got the job done.

I keep telling myself what a wonderful idea micromoves are. My challenge is consistency until the change is permanent. Hearing about the results from Jess's efforts inspired me.

How Do We Create Our Own Micromoves?

We fall into two camps. Some of us over-think and overanalyze our decisions. We want guarantees. A manager I knew used to say, "You want a guarantee, get one for the washing machine." The other group charges ahead with loads of energy, then loses steam. The project is unfinished because they lacked a plan.

For both groups, micromoves are the cure. The analytical over-thinkers find this easy. They devise elaborate lists and micromoves, but then they fail to *act* on them. The second group finds it difficult to plan, but it's easy for them to take a first step. Their challenge is to discipline themselves to remain focused—and finish.

Regardless of your style, take small steps. Take a large project and chunk it down into manageable parts. Micromoves and small steps work for most situations, and more so during a crisis. Done correctly, your brain's flight-or-fight response remains quiet, and you feel less pressured and anxious. The trick is to know yourself well enough to plan micromoves that suit your temperament and energy level.

What Micromoves Work for You?

The smaller the micromove, the better. If your goal is to keep the papers off your desk, filing one document each day (and no more than that) for a week counts as success. For now, ignore the stacks on the floor; you're doing fine. In another week, you'll put two documents away each day. Suddenly you realize you put something away without thinking. You did the micromove, and it's off your plate until the next designated time.

I've got a huge perfectionist streak and make things too complicated for myself. Because I paid for an expensive specialty newsletter, I read it cover to cover and believed it "should" be filed when I'm finished. I used to work as a legal secretary, and old habits are ingrained. In that career, misplacing a document meant possible grounds for a mistrial. The pressure to be exact left its mark.

Despite my attempts with daily filing, I've learned that for me it's better to let the newsletters pile up and sort them every few weeks. Without realizing it, I'm discarding them with no regrets. If I see something pertinent to a current project, I photocopy and file it. Over time, I toss those articles when the project is finished.

Micromoves and tweaks allow you to discover what works for you and not someone else. Instead of letting magazines pile up, a friend of mine looks through them and tears out relevant pages. The rest are recycled the day they appear at her door.

At the oddest moment, an insight for a tiny micromove pops in your mind. Honor it by leaving a voicemail on your smartphone or scribble a note for your PARDA journal. Writing it down reinforces and honors your goals. Your brain loves to be racing and doing something, so use this trait to your advantage. Experiment. Try out your new idea and see if it works. If it doesn't, can it be modified before you give up and discard it?

Circumstances change, yet you cling to old habits that no longer serve you. Adapting or dropping old habits is part of your life cycle.

The Dark Side of Micromoves

It's easy to obsess about getting out the perfect report or sorting papers. Our brains enjoy the immediate sense of fulfillment from completing a task. It doesn't matter if it requires little brainpower, we get it out of the way and feel elated. Those trivial kinds of micromoves engage us. This, in turn, tricks us into doing a bunch of trivial things to experience the completion rush, while important items are left undone. Check in with yourself to ensure your important goals are being met, along with routine tasks that never go away.

With long-term or difficult goals, identify the small steps you have scheduled for yourself and keep moving. Trust the PARDA Process micromoves to take you toward your goals, even when it seems to take forever. Small actions over time result in huge shifts while instilling new habits.

Chapter 11

Ramp It Up

Let's compare micromoves to the fable of the tortoise and the hare. The tortoise plods forward while the hare bounds ahead, then stops, hops, and stops again. Ms. Tortoise won because she was slow and methodical.

But what if we change the story?

While plodding is effective, it isn't always enough. When will you take a risk? You can't be like the tennis player who whacks a tennis ball against an unyielding wall for hours. Eventually, you have to play with a person. Michael Jordan practiced shooting hoops his entire career, but he had to play in hundreds of high-pressure basketball games to hone his skills.

Unless you have a reason to go forward or make a change, your micromoves serve no purpose.

When Will You Take a Risk?

Life has no guarantees of success. The purpose of the PARDA Process is to enable you to create changes that lead to sustained results instead of the frustration of repeated failures. Micromoves are a tool to help you mitigate risk.

Say you've practiced public speaking by speaking up at department meetings. Now you're feeling more confident and chomping at the bit to do more. You deliberately create options to stretch beyond your comfort zone. Perhaps you're forced to take big risks whether you're ready or not. These bigger moves are called "ramp ups."

Just as you planned the micromoves, explore what your big move looks like. Most of the time, this requires focus and building on the micromoves you've already created. By now you've created a consistent habit, and you understand your strengths and vulnerabilities. It's time to move further than ever before.

Ramp-up Spurts

Micromoves happen over time, allowing you to reach your specific "sweet spot" in terms of activity and habits. Experiment by pushing yourself harder for a designated amount of time, then retreat. An example would be forcing yourself to attend events where you don't know anyone but by getting involved, you learn about better job opportunities.

"For me, I like to push myself...I hate feeling complacent, or that I'm not learning." - Derek Hough

The goal is to stretch yourself but not to the point of throwing up your hands and walking away. If that happens, stop. Drop down to an easier micromove and work your way back up—without self-condemnation. You took a risk, and you learned from it—good for you. Celebrate and reward yourself.

What happens when you ramp up your activities? Here's what I concluded after experimenting with a writing binge:

- I discovered my limits.
- If I pushed too hard, I became tired and careless.
- The ramp-ups pushed me over difficult spots.
- If it doesn't work, it's not failure, it's feedback.
- The ramp-up was *my* choice, so I couldn't argue.

A fun way to ramp up is pretending you're getting ready to go on vacation—a time you're willing to work to the point of exhaustion. You finish projects, so your desktop is empty, then you wash your clothes and clean house. Thanks to all this effort, you hit the ground running when you return.

You can't fool yourself forever with this tactic. The novelty wears off, and your body rebels against the pressure. Realize your goal is to feel challenged and satisfied, not burned out. When I've made substantial progress, I reward myself by enjoying dinner out or meeting friends. Then I return to my slower pace and remove the stress.

Other ramp-ups could be adjusting weights or repetitions for a week when you work out. Or you push yourself hard to finish a report sooner than later. You try coding faster—and without losing accuracy. Experiment with pushing yourself beyond your limits for a brief time and monitor the results.

Or do the opposite. If, like me, you push yourself on multiple tasks, then slow down instead. Focus. Why push yourself so hard when you don't have to?

Again, doing ramp-ups are *your* choice.

Once you've finished a ramp-up, use the PARDA Process and analyze the results. **Pause** and **Acknowledge** how it felt to push yourself harder than ever. **Reflect** on what happened. What did you learn? What worked, or what would you do differently? Then **Decide** if you're content with your current pace of activity, or if you will make changes. **Act** on what you learned. You realize that while your ramp-up worked for a short while, it wasn't worth the struggle to do again. And that's okay. Or, to your surprise, you accomplished more than anticipated.

Write brief notes to yourself to cement the learning. Then review them to remind yourself what you've learned for future ramp-ups and goals.

Are You Ready for a Ramp-Up?

The simple answer is "I don't know." Based on experience, when you're ready to ramp it up, go for it—with several caveats. Ask yourself if you've followed through on your micromoves and sustained the change you want. If your goal is to turn in weekly status reports (instead of monthly) and identify new sales prospects, could you continue this for several weeks? Have you learned to feel more confident and/or comfortable with these activities? Is there less struggle for you to maintain the new habit or change than before?

If you have followed through on several linked micromoves as part of your goal, you're ready to take on a ramp-up. However, before you start, be sure you have realistic strategies in place. After steps one, two, and three, do you need options for steps eight, nine, and ten when it's time to move forward?

Ask yourself, "Is this an appropriate stretch?" Wise managers know better than their subordinates when the employees are ready for more responsibility. They assign challenging projects to employees who have met with success when they put forth the extra effort. Now, be your own manager and learn how much you can take on—and when. Don't be surprised if you have unexpected results.

Fiona's Story

Fiona and I met when she called on my previous employer about new office furniture. During our time together, she mentioned she was in a rut at work. As a sales rep for office design and furniture, she was doing okay but wanted to expand in her current situation before deciding to take a different position. We sat down over tea and began to explore. She had already taken time to **Pause** and knew something had to change, but what? She **Acknowledged** her feeling of being stuck in a rut and began to **Reflect** on what to do next.

I started by asking questions. "Do you want to increase sales? Do more networking? Contact previous customers who need new furniture?" Fiona turned inward for a few moments.

"Yeah, I could do all that." Fiona stayed silent, thinking.

"Do you have a routine for your sales calls and networking?"

It turned out Fiona did four or five cold calls each week and was fortunate to have clients who gave her referrals. Unlike Becky, she shrugged. "Those were no big deal, it's a numbers game," she said.

"I hate networking. That's my weak spot." She told me she was an introvert, and while she liked her company's products, going out to "schmooze," as she put it, was hard. I challenged her to a one-month ramp-up. What would happen if she attended more events at her local chamber of commerce? Or took an archery class, something she had enjoyed years ago? At the end of four weeks, she could assess the results.

Fiona wrote down her steps. She would attend meetings and events at her local chamber of commerce at least three times within 30 days. And if she didn't take an archery class for fun, she would rejoin a local nature group that transplanted prairie grass. We agreed she would keep records and report back in a month.

These steps pushed her but not enough for her to give up in frustration. Besides, it took only weeks, not months.

When we met again, she was thoughtful rather than excited.

"I liked seeing former clients at the chamber of commerce, but I'm not sure I want to go every week. It's too much." Attending the prairie grass group was more enjoyable than she'd expected, since she said, "I didn't realize I needed to get out more for me and get away from the city."

She looked at me. "I'm wondering if I should become a group leader, supervising the sales team—maybe move out of calling on clients and into management."

Fiona's ramp-up had unexpected results. Yes, she found she did the sales calls, but being out a couple of times a week for association events was unappealing. Realizing, however, that she wanted a change in responsibilities opened new options.

I don't know what Fiona decided to do, but the ramp-up challenge changed her thinking.

Did You Complete Your Ramp-Up?

How will you know when you're finished your ramp-up? Have you set quantifiable benchmarks to indicate when you're finished? Otherwise, you'll keep getting bogged down and experience a sense of failure. Artistic types are prone to making endless changes to their work. They're nervous about the pain of having their work rejected.

You can't expect perfection or say things like, "I have to lose ten more pounds," or "the files should be in alphabetical order and color-coded." Determine what "good enough" looks like.

If what you attempt doesn't don't turn out as planned, treat yourself with kindness. What if you're exhausted and can't finish the graphics project the same day? Or your plans to remodel the kitchen hit a glitch because there's only enough to cover new cabinets instead of a built-in pantry? It's time to step back, breathe, acknowledge what went wrong, and think about what to do next. Start slowly, with baby steps, then increase your pace and ramp up. Set yourself up for success, not failure.

Ramp-ups taught me that no one can do everything all the time. I must pace myself and stop living life as a perpetual crisis. I hear far too many stories of people who experience catastrophic illness, a death in the family, or other life-changing events. In these cases, people have no choice except to slow down and focus on getting through the day—nothing else.

Chapter 12

Visualization, Positive Thinking, and Law of Attraction

When working with clients and as a librarian, I kept getting questions about the Law of Attraction (LOA), visualization, positive thinking, and the like. People returned the books and told me their lives hadn't changed. Clients needed help picking up the pieces when visualization failed, or they had spent hundreds of dollars on a speaker who promised to help them change their lives—but nothing happened.

Change is hard, so what should they do? To their dismay, they rediscovered there's no quick fix.

You can't go anywhere without seeing books on the law of attraction or visualizing success. Napoleon Hill's *Think and Grow Rich* (1937) is one example; *The Science of Getting Rich* (1910) by Richard Wattles is another. Both are classics in the self-help genre from the 1900s. There's nothing new under the sun, as shown by Esther and Jerry Hicks, who were writing books on the law of attraction during the 1990s. Their book, *Money and the Law of Attraction: Learning to Attract Health, Wealth & Happiness* (2008), made the *New York Times* bestseller list for weeks. There are innumerable YouTube videos and podcasts by life coaches and others touting the virtues of visualization and LOA.

The movie *What the Bleep Do We Know* (also known as What the #$*! Do We (K)now!?) came out in 2004 to huge acclaim. Betsy Chasse, William Arntz, and Mark Vincente wrote, directed, and produced this film, which contained numerous interviews with scientists and leaders extolling the virtues of the law of attraction (LOA) and quantum physics. In 2004, Chasse had it all: She was out of debt, had a wonderful husband, and had directed a film.

Fast forward to 2014. Chasse wrote in her book *Tipping Sacred Cows: The Uplifting Story of Spilt Milk and Finding Your Own Spiritual Path in a Hectic World:*[24]

"Hope without action is like staring at a weight-loss inspired vision board every day while eating a box of glazed donuts."[25]

Her husband was gone and her famous film a memory. She admitted her life was a "hot mess," and she had the hard work of sorting it all out.

Then there's the positive thinking crowd and various religious groups promising health, wealth, and soul mates if one follows the *trend du jour*. Mostly I've shrugged it all off as not being bad—or was it? Recent research has made me wonder.

Athletes Using Visualization

What about those athletes who do mental rehearsals of their moves? Consider the study in which basketball players who visualized shooting baskets performed almost as well as those who practiced daily. It's a classic experiment conducted decades ago at the University of Chicago. But, according to Rebecca Starkey, Librarian for College Instruction and Outreach at The University of Chicago Library, "Our archivists have been unable to find any record for a Dr. Biasotto [or Blaslatto) being affiliated with the University of Chicago."[26] Yet numerous researchers have mentioned this study with no citation to back it up.

Back in the early 1960s, however, there was a "basketball experiment" performed by Professor V. C. Clark of Wayne State University using high school players as subjects over a two-week period. One group practiced free throws in the morning, while another group did "mental practice" but didn't shoot baskets. Both groups did improve their free-throwing skills.

Here's the deal. If visualization enables you to achieve your goals, then keep doing it. Who am I to argue with results? But let's look again at the athletes.

The basketball players who had been practicing physically and *mentally* recalled what they did for successful baskets. They narrowed their sights on free throws and nothing else. Golfers practice a certain part of their golf swing. Swimmers experiment with back flips in the pool to shave seconds off their time. These focused activities sure look like micromoves to me. Further, they represent intense action. Athletes train their bodies to respond a certain way in stressful situations with the goal of making the moves automatic during a game. This is physical practice, not passive visualization.

Visualization versus Practice

Similarly, airline pilots spend countless hours practicing for disaster. If the plane goes into a nosedive, they don't say, "Oh, gee, what should I do?" and thumb through the manual. Their mind and body must respond automatically in an emergency. US Airways pilot Chesley "Sully" Sullenberger landed his plane safely on the Hudson River in New York. The media showed countless images of the passengers lined up on a submerged airplane wing awaiting rescue. This story had a happy ending. Sullenberger himself said he had years of practice getting out of emergencies safely. The flight attendants were experienced in handling tense situations, and ensured passengers remained calm as they waited to leave the plane.

In the medical field, surgeons start as residents assisting and watching veterans. They're allowed to stitch up incisions followed by more challenging steps until they perform an entire operation on their own. When I had surgery a while back, the anesthesiologist asked me if I'd be willing to allow his medical students to observe. I told him, "Of course. But I want assurances *you* are the one keeping me knocked out. I don't want to wake up in the middle of the operation." He reassured me he would do his part, and the students would watch.

When med students start working on patients, professors monitor them closely and intervene if needed. While the thought of having less-skilled professionals work on me seems appalling, I know they aren't left on their own. Having supervised graduate students myself, I knew faculty members didn't allow them to work solo with clients until they've had considerable practice. Based on my own experience, in fact, students were sometimes more cautious and focused than some professionals who'd been working for years.

My advice: Skip visualization and go straight to targeted practice.

Remember my confrontation with Dr. James at the beginning of this book? He hosted a baker's dozen of graduate students in his home to monitor progress on our dissertations. We had to describe what we had done in the prior weeks and commit to our subsequent steps before the next meeting. When we finished, he eased our discouragement by asking us to visualize how it will feel to walk across the stage and receive our colorful doctoral hoods. The hoods are in traditional colors, some of which date back hundreds of years. He used visualization *after* we described our actions toward finishing our dissertation.

"Wake up in the morning, take a couple of deep breaths, close your eyes, and visualize yourself striving, struggling, and then attaining your goal. Picture yourself struggling happily and crossing the finish line." - Brendan Burchard

Visualization of goals does seem to have one helpful benefit. Gabriele Oettingen, whose WOOP strategies were described earlier, ran numerous experiments to see if visualization worked. Yes, it did in a way: subjects who visualized their goals had lower blood pressure. In fact, they were so relaxed, they were less successful than those who made plans and prepared for specific obstacles.

Is Visualization Biblical?

Visualization brings up issues for me as a Christian, however, this isn't the forum to discuss them. The more I examine the practice of visualization, the more uneasy I feel. A major concern is assuming I know what God intends for a situation. When people visualize, they spell out a specific outcome. But what if God has something better in mind? What if something I'm visualizing isn't His will at all?

Another issue is whether I'm trusting that God has the best in mind for me. "For I know the thoughts that I think toward you, says the Lord, thoughts of peace and not of evil, to give you a future and a hope." Jeremiah 29:11 (NKJV) Do I trust in God who knows what's best, when I don't know the outcome? "We walk by faith, and not by sight." (II Corinthians 5:7) Am I willing to walk my talk in faith?

Until modern times when people ventured out after dark, they carried lanterns that glowed a few inches ahead of their steps. We as believers do the same. We move ahead in small steps. Occasionally, God will orchestrate circumstances in which change happens quickly and our lives take an unexpected turn—like turning at a corner we didn't see while walking at night.

Yes, I have a goal in mind. I make plans just like Nehemiah working to rebuild Jerusalem. I must do certain things. But sitting back and passively visualizing the outcome isn't enough.

Positive Thinking: Is It Bad Science?

During the recent twenty or thirty years, a spate of published books and articles have claimed that being happy has health benefits. Newer research is more ambiguous. Some of the early research was downright fraudulent, with results based on the wishful thinking of the researchers.

Sure, we're happier when life goes smoothly. We prefer being around upbeat people. But the pay-off for having happy, positive thoughts with respect to prolonging the life of terminally ill cancer patients dissolved upon further research. According to

James Coyne, Ph.D., a professor of psychology at the University of Pennsylvania, there's no correlation between positive thinking/optimism and cancer survival. In the article "Positive Psychology in Cancer Care: Bad Science, Exaggerated Claims and Unproven Medicine,"[27] Coyne discovered the science was flimsy at best. He and his co-authors challenged positive-thinking researchers to weigh the evidence more carefully.

Apart from the lack of valid scientific support for happiness improving one's life, this denies the reality of what we feel in the moment. Worse, we present a false front to those around us, much like the perfect online profile. How many times have we met people in horrible life situations who say, "Oh, I'm fine, thanks" as they paste a wide smile on their faces. No one wants to admit things are awful for fear of being perceived as whiny or, worse, vulnerable.

In Barbara Fredrickson's book *Positivity: Top-Notch Research Reveals the 3-to-1 Ratio That Will Change Your Life,*[28] the author claimed that having a precise ratio of positive-to-negative frame of mind helps people and companies flourish. She supported this with an elaborate mathematical model from researcher Marcial Losada. *American Psychologist* published their joint paper titled "Positive Affect and the Complex Dynamics of Human Flourishing."[29]

There's a slight problem: Losada's model was gibberish, consisting of mathematics incompatible with the type of research Fredrickson had done. The "positivity ratio" identified by Fredrickson was debunked in an article titled "The Complex Dynamics of Wishful Thinking: The Critical Positivity Ratio."[30]

The lead author of the article questioning Fredrickson's findings was not a professor but a graduate student. To the chagrin of the journal *American Psychologist*, the 2005 article had to be removed. Retraction Watch, a group that monitors scientific research and possible fraud, gave a detailed overview[31] of the concerns expressed by several individuals regarding

Fredrickson's and Losada's work and its partial retraction by the journal.

Barbara Ehrenreich, who wrote *Nickel and Dimed: On (Not) Getting By in America*,[32] penned a biting analysis of the positive thinking movement in America. Some of her statistics are striking. Despite all the emphasis on positive thinking, for example, America ranks twenty-third in self-reported happiness studies.

In her examination of the positive thinking movement in her book *Bright-Sided: How Positive Thinking Is Undermining America*,[33] Ehrenreich explored its history and development in business, religion, and life coaching. She took on the breast cancer "industry" based on her own experience with the disease. She railed against the expectation that those who have cancer need to be bright and cheery while suffering. In her opinion, it's another burden cancer patients don't need to carry.

"Negative thinking can bring about better results when you recognize and then admit the fact that something isn't working." - Bob Knight

Positive thinking causes us to ignore negative thinking that would have resulted in taking less risk. Most people thought real estate would boom until it tanked during the Great Recession of 2008. While many housing markets have recovered since then, a substantial number of people continue to struggle to pay their mortgage because their homes lost value.

Positive Thinking Periodically Trashed Our Economy

In a 2014 study,[34] Gabriele Oettingen and fellow researchers discovered that positive thinking is not the best thing for both the economy and individuals. During the fiscal crisis from 2007 to 2009, the more the newspaper articles in the Economy section of *USA Today* contained positive thinking about the future, the more the Dow Jones Industrial Average *declined* in the subsequent week and one month later. (And yes, the term "positive thinking" is in the original article.) Let me repeat that: thinking positively about the future led to a decline in the Dow Jones Industrial Average.

The researchers also examined presidential inaugural speeches. The more positive thinking about the future from the president, the more the gross domestic product and employment rate declined during their presidencies. This effect went all the way back to the New Deal in the 1930s. The authors of the article concluded, "In the present research, positive thinking about the future expressed in newspaper articles and presidential addresses predicted economic downturn in a society."

Now, there's nothing intrinsically wrong with happiness and positive thinking. Denying the reality of problems and suffering, however, diminishes thousands of years of human struggle. Staying focused on positive thinking results in avoiding those who are hurting and, in so doing, undermine their human dignity at a time when they need it most.

Happiness and Health

Do feelings of happiness help you live longer if you're healthy, and not ill? A study[35] published in 2015 in the British medical journal *The Lancet* followed one million middle-aged British women for ten years. "Happiness and related measures of well-being do not appear to have any direct effect on mortality," the researchers concluded. A "substantial minority" of healthy British women said they were stressed or unhappy, but over the next decade, they were no more likely to die than were the women who were generally happy. Furthermore, the study found that women in poor health felt unhappy and stressed, but there was no direct effect of unhappiness on their rates of death. The conclusion? Being unhappy doesn't seem to directly cause disease.

Negativity Isn't All Bad

Listening to my dad argue back and forth with himself when I was a kid was enlightening. I learned he wasn't afraid to explore the downside of his choices. Looking ahead and planning for the worst alerts people to the pitfalls along the way.

Susan David, in her book *Emotional Agility: Get Unstuck, Embrace Change and Thrive in Work and Life,*[36] lists several benefits to having unpleasant moods. When we're in a bad mood, we're more careful and less gullible than when we're feeling upbeat. Those in bad moods are better at crafting arguments to sway others to their point of view. Negativity helps us persevere. These findings tell us to use our bad moods as another resource for achieving results.

By acknowledging your negative and "not nice" parts, you honor all your feelings, not just the "good" ones or what others think is acceptable. When we focus on one emotion, whether positive, negative, or something in between, we risk cutting off valuable data. Furthermore, we're choosing not to honor the full range of our personality.

Chapter 13

Where Do You Go from Here?

I've struggled, researched, and strategized to find ways to change my own habits and achieve goals. Positive thinking makes me all warm and fuzzy inside (and scientists have confirmed that visualization in and of itself makes you more relaxed), but my challenge was to change for real.

I've procrastinated starting projects because I didn't know what to do or felt scared. I could visualize my goals, but as Oettingen pointed out, I became less motivated to put forth the effort. I've created elaborate plans, then felt intimidated by the magnitude of what I was trying to accomplish.

Now, instead of beating myself up, I have strategies to get me over the hump. Before I dive into something, I make plans then take small, consistent steps. My life isn't perfect, but I'm more at peace. I don't beat myself up as much if I mess up.

Waiting

Being patient with discomfort, paradox, and absence of clear answers challenges us. It's too easy to become discouraged. A sign of maturity is being able to tolerate the discomfort of ambiguity and uncertainty. Doing micromoves will teach patience if we let it. In a society where everything is instantaneous, we've lost the art of waiting. Our grandparents would say, "Rome wasn't built in a day." How much are we willing to wait for the results of our efforts?

The longer we walk with the Lord, read Scriptures, and spend time listening to solid preaching, the easier it becomes to discern what God would have us do. Still, I look back on my life and question why God had me in situations that strained my health and sanity. I have to trust God that I made the right decision at the time since no red flags appeared. No guarantees exist that everything will turn out as planned.

"God doesn't guarantee you won't fail." - Ronald Larson

Angry people have glared at me and complained that, despite their plans and efforts, things didn't work out. I get that; I planned to be a university professor, but by the time I graduated with my degrees, several hundred colleges and universities had closed. Job openings were scarce or non-existent. The situation is even more dire today, and to make things worse, students are saddled with thousands of dollars of debt.

What about those who have lost everything through no fault of their own? How many men and women have prayed for a loving spouse and marriage, but their prayers went unheard? Despite their best efforts, they lost a job or a coveted position. And doing all the steps of the PARDA Process is no guarantee their efforts will turn out as planned. What then?

Several of my professional career dreams never materialized, nor did my husband and I have children. I've lost family and friends to death, and I miss them. There have been problems and sickness. "Why, Lord?" I cry out in grief. Either I trust God during periods of doubt, or I let bitterness fester in my soul.

Some Christians come to me in tears after marrying someone who later walked out on their marriage. When we explored their choices, we had no clue why this hadn't worked out. Dedicated missionaries experience mental or physical breakdowns in the mission field. Does that mean they misunderstand God's call for them? We figure if we're good little Christian boys and girls, we'll be immune from tragedy. Things will always turn out right—until they don't. I've sat with weeping, angry Christians trying to make sense of it all. I've thought long and hard about these situations and reached these four conclusions.

First, there are no guarantees. God will never leave or forsake us, but people do. Yes, people let us down, double-cross us, and fail us. Jesus was well-acquainted with betrayal. One disciple (Judas) turned him over to the authorities while another (Peter) denied he knew Him, and three times at that. Another (John) ran away.

If I prayerfully sought God's will and consulted with multiple believers, I had to go on the information I had available at the time.

Second, we all grow and change. A job that used to suit us before now seems stale. When we figured the job was there until retirement, our whole department got outsourced. We must allow for circumstances and personal development. Life doesn't stop.

Third, tragedy happens. Forest fires have wiped out homes of believers and unbelievers alike. Hurricanes have leveled neighborhoods. God did not reach down and put out the fires or stop the winds. In His providence and mercy, a few homes were spared. There's a reason they're called miracles—they don't happen often. In the book of Acts, Peter was led out of prison by an angel, while a chapter or two earlier, James, the brother of the Apostle John, had his head chopped off. How did those early believers make sense of this tragedy?

Fourth, we walk by faith and not by sight. It is a decision on my part, granted by God's grace, to choose to trust Him in the dark times of my life. I don't always feel like loving Him. I weep. But do I still trust Him? YES. Do I believe He is sovereign in my life and knows what is best? YES. I'm less than honest, however, if I claim I never have doubts. I've told friends and loved ones that when I get to Heaven, I'll have tons of questions.

What if there is no desirable solution? We work with what we know and have while we trust God to work *with* and *for* us in each situation. The PARDA Process, for me and others, is a tool, not an answer.

Regrets are Futile

Do you ever wonder "what if?" The next time it happens, stop. If I had taken a job offer from IBM back in the day, I could have been transferred all over the world. What if I had married someone else instead of Ron, the man who's been my husband for many years? Guess what? Regardless of the decision, I would have had experiences and problems involving other people and circumstances. Not better or worse, but different. Today, I'm profoundly grateful I married Ron.

When we pray about our choices, seek counsel, and then move out in faith, we've made the best decision we could make at the time. We may wish we had done things differently, but what's the point of wishing? We mentally replay our choices, but we live with the consequences of our decisions.

"I made decisions that I regret, and I took them as learning experiences.... I'm human, not perfect, like anybody else." - Queen Latifah

Revisit and revise your regret loops. Apply the PARDA Process and decide how you would handle the same situation if it arose again. Some men and women make the same poor choices in picking partners time and again. Friends shake their heads but nothing they say makes a difference. Then they wake up, seek counseling, and identify why they make their faulty choices. What happens? They slip again into a wrong relationship, but it lasts for two weeks instead of months because they catch their mistake early and minimize the damage.

Can I Let It Go?

Looking back, I see how I had planned, but God allowed circumstances beyond my control to change what happened. On the one hand, I needed to create my strategies and micromoves. On the other, I must be willing to let go and whisper, "Lord, Your will be done, not mine."

We must pause and acknowledge our anger and resentment regarding unsettling experiences, not stuff down painful thoughts. This might be sufficient to calm us down and let us think more clearly. Realizing we're in the grip of strong emotions reminds us not to make decisions we might later regret.

While I've been unhappy with the way some goals turned out, I'm immeasurably blessed with loving friends and family. I have a roof over my head and a job. I'm healthy. God has saved and kept me through it all, good and bad. This is where my journal has been invaluable. I reread earlier entries and marvel at how much has worked out for the best.

The prophet Habakkuk lived in a time like ours when injustice was rampant and evil people appeared to prosper. Worse, God hid His face. Where was He? Despite all the problems, Habakkuk ended the book that bears his name with this haunting close: (Habakkuk 3:17-18, NASB)

> Though the fig tree may not blossom,
> Nor fruit be on the vines;
> Though the labor of the olive may fail,
> And the fields yield no food;
> Though the flock may be cut off from the fold,
> And there be no herd in the stalls—
> Yet I will exult in the LORD,
> I will rejoice in the God of my salvation.

Embrace Change

People have suggested I consciously embrace change, and they're right. But I don't *like* a lot of change. Now an adult, I'm getting better at letting things go and loosening my attachment to stability. When I realized I could swap all-or-nothing thinking for smaller changes at my own pace, the world didn't fall apart. And the large, unexpected adjustments didn't seem as awful because of it.

Two kinds of change exist: 1) those we anticipate to some extent and 2) others that are unexpected.

The kinds of things we anticipate include:

- Your child grows and enters a new grade annually.
- In many places, there's a rhythm to the seasons.
- Your company has a rhythm tied to projects and events.
- Your new home will be finished by a certain date.
- Your body will change as you age.

Then there are changes we don't expect:

- You're laid off and never saw it coming.
- Your marriage ends.
- You get a life-threatening diagnosis from your doctor.
- You have a spate of home repairs that drain your bank account.

Digging in my heels doesn't work. I whine and kick the furniture, but I can't stop change. I throw my hands up and restart my PARDA Process again and again. In so doing, the PARDA Process strikes a balance between endless thinking versus rushing into action.

Pause and step back with a few breaths or time away to return refreshed.

Acknowledge mixed emotions and let them wash through our bodies without beating ourselves up.

Reflect on what happened and observe what is going on right now.

Decide and define micromoves, obstacles, and a plan.

Act on the next step, including a micromove.

Repeat as needed again and again.

The past is a seductive place to visit but a lousy place to live. We moan and say, "Things are awful." We mope over losses and refuse to let them go. I challenge myself to move on. I mourn familiar places that are no more. Bookstores I've loved have closed, while favorite loved ones and friends have died. It's my choice to stay stuck or move on. I tell myself the future will offer new possibilities.

"Changes and progress very rarely are gifts from above. They come out of struggles from below." - Noam Chomsky

I winced when the landscaper chopped and pruned the huge lilac bush in the side yard outside my kitchen. The familiar scent didn't waft through my window for two years. This year, the bush is overflowing with purple blossoms, and I inhale their scent. In the time since the landscaper whacked off its branches, I've made new friends and became involved in different activities. Painful events in my own life have transmuted into something better once I allowed myself to let them go.

Ecclesiastes 3:1-8 (NKJV, italics in the original) reminds us:

To everything there is a season,
    A time for every purpose under heaven:
A time to be born,
    And a time to die;
A time to plant,
    And a time to *pluck* what is planted;
A time to kill,
    And a time to heal;
A time to break down,
    And a time to build up;
A time to weep,
    And a time to laugh;
A time to mourn,
    And a time to dance;
A time to cast away stones,
    And a time to gather stones;
A time to embrace,
    And a time to refrain from embracing;
A time to gain,
    And a time to lose;
A time to keep,
    And a time to throw away;

A time to tear,
　　And a time to sew;
A time to keep silence,
　　And a time to speak;
A time to love,
　　And a time to hate;
A time of war,
　　And a time of peace.

These timeless words summarize the flow of human life and its challenges. May you use the PARDA Process to flow in your periods of reflection and activity.

Part II

Using the PARDA Process
in Your Life

What do you choose to examine when you start the PARDA Process? Anywhere you want—experiment. Start, and if you don't feel like doing all the steps at once, that's fine. Or take a few minutes and then delve deeper. Make sure you do both the thinking and action steps for effective results. Grab a notebook or sketch pad and make notes. I sound like a broken record, but you'll find that writing deepens and enriches the experience. The more you use the PARDA Process, the sooner it will become a part of your interior repertoire for navigating life.

The PARDA Process is always available—don't wait for the "perfect moment." We don't eat once but again and again in a variety of circumstances. Change is continual, whether you want it to be or not.

While you've read examples of the PARDA Process, why not explore *your* good times and make them better? Ask yourself, "What went right? What made this experience enjoyable or satisfying? How do I bring more joy/satisfaction/peace into my life?" Use the PARDA process to figure things out, write down your thoughts, and implement your ideas.

People ask me if they should save their writings. That's up to you. I think it's best to have them all in one place and refer to them. I've found myself re-examining earlier events to discern patterns when situations appear to repeat themselves.

However, with respect to my earlier comments about spewing your dirtiest, darkest thoughts onto paper, you might want to shred or destroy those pages—it's up to you. With writing dumps, it's tempting to think they must be perfect. Not at all.

Leave in the misspellings and the four-letter words. Dump it all out. No one will see these pages except you. Use your journal as a holding place for your thoughts, ideas, and feelings.

It's imperative to have a safe place to vent, and your PARDA Process journal is the venue for writing down all the stuff you can't say in the heat of the moment. If you have snoopy roommates, children, or spouse, find a hiding spot. My mom used to stash cookies (wrapped in several clean, empty plastic bread bags) in the dirty laundry basket, knowing no one would burrow through dirty underwear and stinky socks.

Topics such as money, relationships, and your job are too broad to address in one sitting. Trust those micromoves. Choose one aspect to work on, then go to the next. Do short stints and work where you're undisturbed. Return to earlier writings to see if there's another issue. Don't overthink, just write. The questions become jumping-off points—and you'll have more questions pop up.

Using a timer helps, since the exploration is limited to a few minutes. Only you can judge how hard to push but do push yourself to get past the initial wave of unpleasant emotions. It's important to have compassion for yourself, just as you would for an unhappy toddler or a close friend.

Read (or at least skim) the chapters that follow for examples. While the steps have the same sequence from **Pause** to **Act**, there are no right or wrong answers. The PARDA Process works better with a little preparation, which will focus your efforts.

While I urge you to keep a record, not all sessions require pages of notes if you don't want them. A little something is always better than nothing:

- Find a place where you'll be undisturbed at least thirty minutes.
- Turn off your phone and other electronic devices.
- Proactively deal with potential distractions, including pets.

- Write down the date for future reference.
- Take a few minutes to breathe and settle in.
- Set a timer and write without stopping for 15-20 minutes until it rings.
- Let mistakes and bad language go—get it all down.
- Be playful, gentle, and compassionate with yourself.

When you've finished writing, take some breaths and **Pause**. **Acknowledge** your efforts. **Reflect** on what you discovered in your writing and **Decide** what you want to do next. Identify your micromoves and set up the date and time you plan to **Act**. I chose the following categories because I've either worked on them myself, or people have asked me for help.

- Relationship challenges
- Work and career
- Overwhelm
- Money and debt
- Joy and play

Needless to say, there are many more topics. What do you want to examine? Have fun and be kind.

Chapter 14

Relationship Challenges

Life's great when you love your family, your job, and the neighbor's pit bull who barks all night. If you are in a sticky relationship situation—be it with your manager, neighbor, or loved one—proceed cautiously. Use the PARDA Process to explore your unpleasant experiences. It won't be enjoyable, but it will defuse emotions and let you detach enough for insight to come through.

Don't try to do it all at once. Take tiny steps. Be peaceful with not having a solution right this minute. Since change is inevitable, you'll find a new job or roommate, or you'll progress in another fashion. Start by examining your relationship with one problematic person in your life.

But before you begin, do the preparation described at the beginning of Part II.

Turn to the PARDA Process

Pause by taking some breaths and become calm. Think about someone you can't avoid, no matter what. Take a few deep breaths and relax. What emotions do you feel toward this person—anger, fear, hatred? Which one dominates?

Where do you sense your emotions in your body? Do your shoulders tighten? Does your jaw clench when you think of this person? Sense those areas in your body and focus on relaxing them.

Acknowledge your dislike, anger, or other unpleasant emotions. Be honest and admit without shame what you're feeling. Scribble out your nastiest thoughts as I did about Randy.

Keep writing for fifteen or twenty minutes. If feelings keep coming up, keep writing. No one will see these pages and getting emotions on paper removes them from your body and mind.

We are ashamed to admit hating someone. We grit our teeth and try not to envy the person who was promoted in our place or has a new car while we drive a clunker. Feelings of anger and hate have been part of the human condition for millennia. Look at one of the so-called "imprecatory psalms" in which David spills out his desire for someone in authority to die, with his children left as orphans. (Psalm 108) Here was a man after God's own heart, and he struggled with hatred like the rest of us.

Let the "he said/she said" conversations repeat in your mind without judgment. Write them down. Allow yourself to explore being angry and defensive; keep writing until the timer goes off. When you don't know what to say, write that you don't know what to say or repeat the last several words you scribbled. Take some breaths and relax. Stretch and get a drink of water.

"Nothing is perfect. Life is messy. Relationships are complex. Outcomes are uncertain. People are irrational." - Hugh Mackay

Reflect on what you've written. Highlight or underline sections that trigger your ire. While doing this, explore the history of the relationship. Was there a betrayal? Is there a painful issue that was never resolved, such as a financial problem?

Do another writing dump, and this time explore what was going on *around* the event. If your ex-spouse didn't pay child support, for example, might there be another reason besides spitefulness, such as unemployment or prolonged illness? You don't have to condone what happened but do allow for possible alternatives. Do your best to reflect on your part in the situation and be vulnerable.

Do understand that those who give you grief won't change as much as you might hope? If they make a good-faith effort, chances are it won't continue. It isn't part of their nature to be less demanding or stop screaming when you make small mistakes. If you are unable to change or leave the situation for the time being, how will you cope? Do you have support strategies to maintain your health and sanity?

This kind of exploration is hard, painful work. One advantage to writing it down is being able to put your journal aside and return a day or two later to review it. Record new realizations in the interim and explore. Please be compassionate with yourself.

Decide what to do next. You fantasize about poisoning your neighbor's noisy dog and feel guilty—that's the wrong solution. What is your desired outcome? You and your neighbor may not become best buds, but what about talking calmly about how much the dog barks? What micromoves would shift things, even a little?

Act with a micromove. An excellent start would be to gather information. Meet with a close friend whose opinion you respect. Decide how you will interact with the neighbor, coworker, or other person who is giving you grief. With pressure at home or work, take care of yourself. Exercise, knowing a twenty-minute walk at lunch or after dinner will lighten your mood.

It takes courage to explore your relationships, and it's challenging to first identify and then make minor changes. Use the PARDA Process while striving for healing and resolution.

Chapter 15

Work and Career

Whether job seekers are recent grads or laid-off executives, innumerable books, websites, and organizations exist for assistance. If you're seeking work, ask your local library, social services agency, or employment office for suggestions.

No matter how many resources are available, a job search is never easy. I suggest you use the PARDA Process to clarify your thoughts during this time. Do you feel bitter about not having more interviews? Blame your boss for promoting someone else? Examine both your thoughts and feelings. If you're vague about what's important to you beyond a paycheck, ponder what you *don't* want and change it around to its positive opposite. I dislike answering telephones and dealing with innumerable interruptions while writing a difficult report. When flipped around, this looks like I prefer a position where I focus on assignments while someone else deals with the phones and questions.

Give yourself time. Finding new employment doesn't happen quickly. Include the PARDA Process as part of your overall search strategy.

Before you start, do the preparation described at the beginning of Part II.

Turn to the PARDA Process

Pause for a few moments and focus on your employment situation. Keep a pen or pencil and paper nearby to write down your thoughts and ideas. Let tension drain from your shoulders and other parts of your body. Is there a strong feeling or thought that keeps popping up? Relief that the axe fell after months of uncertainty? Wondering how you will pay the bills? Write down all that you're sensing. Dump it all out.

Acknowledge your present circumstances. Were you laid off unexpectedly? Do you feel bored and restless but don't know why? Should you be thinking about a new job or changing careers if your current position has benefits and pays the bills? What thoughts are going through your head?

What sensations are in your body and where? Tightness in your shoulders? Queasy stomach? Let the words spill out. Write whatever you think without stopping or evaluating. Include your rotten feelings, misspelled words, and nasty thoughts. When you're stuck, repeat the last few words or the whole sentence. More material will arise when you push past the initial five or ten minutes.

Resist the temptation to check social media, delete emails, or find other distractions when your discomfort increases. You will use all sorts of excuses to avoid your job search rather than sit in the unpleasantness. Do the writing anyway.

Once you have finished, move. Get up. Stretch. How do you feel now? Relieved that everything's out in the open? Drained because you didn't realize how much you hated your current position? Terrorized because you wonder if you'll find any job at your age?

If you're working but feel dissatisfied, what changes do you want to make? Have your friends or significant made suggestions?

Start the next step after a short break or better, a day later. When insights show up unexpectedly, jot them down.

Reflect on whatever thoughts arise without judgment. Tell yourself it's safe to realize how much you dislike your current job and the anxiety of making a change. Make notes listing what you want/don't want in the next position and use them in your next writing dump to clarify your ideas.

"The most common way people give up their power is by thinking they don't have any." - Alice Walker

Suddenly, you find yourself updating your résumé or creating a new one. What about calling an old boss who moved to another company? Take a closer look at current job postings in your field? Write down all your ideas, because if you don't capture them, you'll lose these insights. Ponder your next micromove. Doing so doesn't have to commit you to change if you're not ready. Besides, your brain, which loves a challenge, will generate more ideas.

Keep writing down your ideas and put them in sequence. What do you need to do first? Do you need to update your skills? Revise your résumé? Revise your LinkedIn profile?

While you wrote, you realized there were aspects of your job you enjoyed. How do you increase those activities and delegate others? Is it better to stay, rather than leave?

Decide your next step or, at most, two of them. Avoid creating an elaborate plan, and instead, allow flexibility. Explore potential obstacles and fears. What motivates you to keep going despite challenges? Do you prefer to remain in your current position? Do you need additional training? Some employees make career-building changes and then reassess their choices.

Act by identifying one or two micromoves and complete them. They can be as simple as setting up an appointment with a colleague at a different company or becoming more involved in an association. Write down the date and time you plan to do research or call a contact. When you complete these steps, choose your next micromove.

Be discreet about your plans, especially if you're still employed. Use your own devices, not the computer in the office, to update your information. Use your cell phone during lunch or after hours. Be a hard worker up until your last day. Your boss doesn't need to know until you give notice. Good luck!

Chapter 16

Overwhelm

When we meet with friends, the first thing we say after hello is "How's it going?" The inevitable litany begins: "What a busy time at work. Michael and Jenn are keeping us on the go with all their sports activities. I can't seem to get caught up."

Do we flaunt how busy we are as a status symbol? Online sites make it worse when you read the list of accomplishments on a friend's page. You wonder what's wrong, because it seems as though you can't accomplish a thing compared to your buddies.

I used to think overwhelm was a female issue, but now I see young men opening up about the clash they experience between work and family life. More men are responsible for childcare (if not housework) and do yard work or shopping. Both men and women are stressed in their life roles.

Unless we stop and take a hard look at our lives, our bodies and life challenges will do it for us. Doing housework goes to the bottom of the list if your child or loved one lands in the hospital. Worse is when *you* are the one in the hospital after you missed the last stair step while racing to your car to make up for being late.

Before you start, do the preparation described at the beginning of Part II.

Turn to the PARDA Process

Pause for a few minutes and breathe. Grab your notebook and go to a coffee shop or library to reduce distractions. For now, put everything aside and let tension drain from your body. Allow it to ooze out of your neck and shoulders. Is this the first time in days (weeks) you've slowed down? If you're exhausted to the point that you struggle to stay awake let alone take the subsequent steps, stop. Do the PARDA Process at another time. Instead, take your exhaustion as an urgent warning to slow down and nurture yourself. Caring for a new baby or starting a new job (to name two challenges of many) usually causes feelings of overwhelm. Give yourself time and make a list of what you need to do. Take it easy.

You realized you're in over your head. Or you're panicked at the number of commitments you've taken on and struggle to keep up with them. Has living in overwhelm been your default mode and you've reached the end of your rope? If so, you will need different strategies to change the habits that got you in this mess in the first place.

Acknowledge your thoughts and fears that you'll never get caught up. Dump all the anger, frustration, and resentment into your notebook and then observe your guilt and shame without judgment. Have compassion and stop beating yourself up. Set the timer for fifteen minutes and write what's going on. Is it job stress? Coming home exhausted to your spouse and children and other responsibilities? Keeping up with the kids' activities? It was fun at first, but now attending them has become a burden, and you feel guilty for admitting it.

I've seen people cry when they start to explore the tension and stress they'd stuffed down. If that describes you, let the tears roll and keep writing. If the timer goes off and you want to keep scribbling, do it. Again, resist the temptation to check social media, delete emails, or find other distractions when your discomfort increases. Keep scribbling until your timer rings.

Once you have finished, move. Get up. Stretch. How do you feel? The temptation is to walk away. Do the following instead.

Reflect on what you wrote. Chances are, the strongest concern will rise to the top—be it home, work, or a special project. Identify critical issues and separate them into categories. What are your priorities? When you look closer, is it the stuff at home or at work creating the most havoc? Where is there the biggest bang for the buck in terms of change with the least amount of effort?

Start making notes and have compassion on yourself for letting things reach this point. List specific challenges such as credit card debt, long hours at work, and care of elderly parents. If a task like laundry or cleaning the fish tank bugs you but seems trivial, write it down anyway. Was there a time when you were less stressed? Did an event shove you into overwhelm, or did it creep in before you realized it?

"Today I escaped from the crush of circumstances, or better put, I threw them out, for the crush wasn't from outside me but in my own assumptions." - Marcus Aurelius

Everyone has different stressors, and these change with life stages. A woman with two toddlers under the age of four has hands-on care of little ones who demand constant attention. They can't feed or dress themselves without her help. Housework becomes minimal. Now more dads are staying home and taking over childcare while mom works. They are shocked at the amount of effort involved in taking care of children.

The combination of having teenagers and elderly parents pose different challenges. Moms and dads serve as chauffeurs for both generations as they try to juggle everyone's needs. Their marriage and health suffer.

What next? If you have a few extra dollars in your budget, hire household help for a few hours a week. If you have more time than money, learn how to make double batches of favorite meals and freeze them. Determine what's important versus urgent among your responsibilities. Paring down debt takes precedence over replacing a worn rug. Discern what works for you, not your friends.

There is no quick fix for overwhelm. You'll find clusters of small tweaks when you explore what can be eliminated, simplified, or delegated. Sit down with everyone and explain what you need. Start teens and tweens clearing the dinner table and doing their own laundry. Can they rotate chores? Make realistic commitments, and let the rest go.

If work is keeping you swamped, are there templates or standardized procedures? Write down any ideas, no matter how silly. What about relationship conflicts or unreal expectations zapping your energy?

Decide what to tackle first. Start with one—and only one—problem. Trying to fix too many things at once will shove you back into overload paralysis. For the first time, you understand the enormity of your stressors, and it's scary.

Most important, identify a few minutes for yourself, be it a long, hot bath, or listening to music before bedtime.

Act on one micromove. A trivial step (e.g., teaching your children how to set the table) takes time at first, but frees you from a task and allow you to start dinner earlier. Once they've set the table properly for two weeks, give them another assignment. Show them how to scrape their plates and take them to the sink.

At work, do something as simple as postponing emails for an hour or two and dive into projects instead. Turn off the notifications, commit to doing batches of emails three times daily, and stick to it. Switching back and forth between emails and activities wastes time and decreases productivity.

Keep asking questions like these and let the answers flow. What reports or meetings should be streamlined or eliminated? What if you met with coworkers, spouse, or significant other and asked for specific help? People are usually helpful if you level with them about what you need. And if they can't help, ask them for suggestions.

Overwhelm is endemic, and we see it manifested in fatigue, irritability, and a sense that we're out of control. Unfortunately, if we don't let ourselves slow down, our bodies will do it for us. That's when we'll have no choice but to rest and let our obligations pile up. Head off this undesirable result by using the

PARDA Process to make your life more manageable and enjoyable.

Chapter 17

Your Relationship with Money

Money is a challenging topic for the best of us, entangled as it is with our upbringing, emotions, and experiences. Two people in a relationship each bring a background in finances and they need to work as a team, but few receive any help doing so. Whether single or married, financial issues pack a wallop. As financial columnist Peter Dunn ("Pete the Planner") wrote, "No, your financial life is not about money. It's about behavior."[37] How right he is.

Money issues run the gamut from paying off debt to learning that "budget" isn't a dirty word. Your concerns might include such things as setting priorities or living on one income. Here, I use debt because it's a huge issue for so many people.

"Remove falsehood and lies far from me;
Give me neither poverty nor riches—
Feed me with the food allotted to me;
Lest I be full and deny You,
And say, "Who is the Lord?"
Or lest I be poor and steal,
And profane the name of my God." - Proverbs 30:8-9

Most people have a few positive memories around money. Maybe you saved months for a special event or scraped up enough money for a new car. How were you able to do that, and could you do it again? Experiment with the money games in Chapter 9 and explore what's going well in your relationship with money by seeking the smallest positive experience. Use the PARDA Process to address whatever aspects of money and finances you're experiencing.

The 2016 real median earnings of men and women who worked full-time, year-round were $51,640 and $41,554, respectively, not statistically different from their 2015 estimates.[38]

Recent U.S. government Census figures report that American families have an average annual income of $52,000, while individual incomes are $28,000. (These figures are based on what the majority of citizens must pay into Social Security and don't include people who are paid "under the table.") Let's stir the pot. Students have one trillion dollars in school loan debt that cannot be discharged in bankruptcy. And according to a study[39] by the Harvard Medical School, more than half of the bankruptcies occur due to medical bills. In 2016, NerdWallet published a detailed study[40] of how much debt the average American carries, starting with over $16,000 in credit card debt.

Before we start judging ourselves and others for being too deep in debt, stop. Note that, over time, the cost of living has increased, but wages haven't kept pace. Families with children find it hard to make ends meet, while the self-employed who aren't covered by an employer's health plan are in a bind. Most of us feel a deep sense of shame and embarrassment about our money situation.

It's too easy to shove the bills in the drawer yet again and then wonder why you have difficulty sleeping. First, do these exercises by yourself before involving your partner or spouse. Decide you won't play the blame game, either toward yourself or anyone else.

Before you start, do the preparation described at the beginning of Part II.

Turn to the PARDA Process

Pause and take a few calming breaths. Identify one narrow area of struggle with respect to your finances. If you can't keep track of your receipts, for example, start with that. Feel the fear and tension in your body and decide to let it go for now.

Acknowledge your thoughts and feelings, including ones that are uncomfortable. Date a fresh page in your notebook or journal and scribble a few words. Anger? Fear? Do words like "terrified" or phrases like "we'll never get out of this hole" come to mind? Where in your body do you sense the strongest emotions? Does your stomach ache? Is your chest getting tight or your head throbbing? Acknowledge your feelings of shame or guilt without blaming yourself. Pour out your inner dialogue, including phrases such as "How could I let this happen?" Feel free to cry.

Keep writing for at least fifteen minutes without censoring your thoughts or worrying about spelling and grammar. If you want to keep writing when the timer goes off, do so. While you're writing, suspend any judgment. This is not the time to beat yourself up.

Stop and drink water. Stretch. Step away from your writing, regardless of how you feel. Don't go back and reread what you wrote; you'll want to scratch out what seems too raw. Instead, turn to a fresh page.

After you finish writing, **Reflect** on your thoughts. Get your emotions out of the way as you jot down ideas. Perhaps you could disconnect the cable TV and use a dedicated line for internet access. You realize you and your spouse spend money when you've had a disagreement or a rotten day at work to unwind. How could the two of you change that?

What is your spending profile? Does money dribble away because of weekly lunches out or Friday drinks with coworkers? Some are "good" about saving for a while, then oops, a big splurge, much like blowing a diet.

Make a list of your debt categories. Are you carrying student loans? What about medical bills? Or credit card debt, the costliest form because of the high interest rates? Then go on a cash diet (no credit cards) and locate reputable debt counseling services for assistance.

Are there any patterns in your life you where you overspend? Even better, are there places where you don't have a money problem? Compared to my friends, I've never been enamored of new shoes. But turn me loose in a bookstore, and I can spend the equivalent of two pairs of high-end leather boots in less than fifteen minutes.

What are your earliest memories around money? When I was a little girl, I recall how scared and small I felt when Mom and I walked into the bank. This was one of those old ornate buildings with large pillars and marble desks on which to write deposit slips. When she plopped me on the hard ledge next to the teller, the marble felt cold and hard on my bottom and legs. After taking a check from my mother, the teller counted out cash and shoved it through a small metal hollow under the barred, glass window. Everyone spoke softly and sounds echoed, getting lost in the room's lofty ceilings.

To this day, I'm still intimidated by banks and financial issues. I must push myself to be more aware of how to deal with money. Do you have similar memories? Write them down, because they still carry an emotional charge for you today.

Think about how your parents handled the family's finances while you were growing up. What did you learn about them? Did your parents squabble on payday? I can't stress enough bringing out all your memories and emotions around finances. You and your partner both bring individual money histories to the table, and you need to come together and create your joint financial style. If you're married or engaged, I urge you and your significant other to sit down and talk about your financial arrangements. An impartial friend or trusted advisor can listen to both of you describe your money challenges and make suggestions.

Going into debt doesn't occur in isolation. If you don't get to the root of the problem, you'll find it difficult to dig yourself out. Then you'll fall back into the same old habits.

Decide on your next step. For some, taking out credit card bills and tallying the amount due is all they can handle. That's fine, but then what? Start by listing places for information and support. Find a time when you and your spouse or partner will agree to meet to discuss what's going on around money. Have a cup of coffee at a local eating spot where you won't be overheard. Meeting outside the home helps to level the playing field and keeps emotions in check.

Use the acronym HALT, which stands for Hungry, Angry, Lonely, and Tired. HALT means to stop and take care of these basic human needs when you become aware of them—especially before you do something important. Thus, avoid money conversations when you're tired, hungry, or angry.

Keep the discussion short and simple by taking ownership of your own mistakes first. Always avoid blame. Regardless of how much money you have, set up a game plan to stay on the same page and continue to work as a team.

What is your initial micromove? Eliminating two or three lattés a week and substituting home-brewed coffee stored in a thermos would free up nine or ten dollars a week without making you feel deprived.

Act by choosing a micromove, then write down the date and time when you plan to carry it out. Be proactive and identify what derails you. Perhaps experiment with if-then statements. *"If* I'm tempted to buy an item on sale, *then* I will leave the store and shop my closet at home."

Always affirm your small victories. Praise yourself when you complete a micromove. Yes, it feels silly, but it reworks the tapes in your head.

While the PARDA Process is an excellent start, find help for yourself if money issues threaten to derail your life.

Chapter 18

Joy and Play

It's easy to get wrapped up in the busyness of our lives. We're told to "stop and smell the roses" (something I hate to do because their smell reminds me too much of funerals), but when do we take time for pleasure and fun? I'm not talking about vacations, they happen too seldom for most of us. But what simple, everyday things buoy our spirits and minimize burnout?

As noted earlier, my temperament is to go, go, go, crash—go, go, crash. It has always been a challenge to pace myself. Once I start cleaning house and filing paperwork, I'm on a roll. How quickly I forget that if I do too much, I'm exhausted and don't recover quickly.

The temptation for many is to meet the needs of others first, leaving scant crumbs of time and energy for themselves. How do you replenish yourself before you drive yourself to exhaustion? Can you do this without feeling guilty?

The PARDA Process has taught me to savor small pleasures. Believe me, I'm a work in progress. Yet, by using these five steps, I've uncovered surprising moments of contentment and enjoyment.

I love to stroll along Lake Michigan, although I need most of a day to drive to and from, find a parking space, and then take time and unwind. My other pleasures? An hour or two browsing new and used bookstores is a real treat. Ditto for catching up on emails from friends or stroking the animals at a dog or cat show.

Challenge yourself to create a list of satisfying activities. When you're feeling restless and edgy, you don't want to draw a blank on your options. Decide which activities need more of your time. If you enjoy knitting, crafts, or handwork, set up a space where you grab a few creative moments without taking everything out or putting it away. When your crafts are close at hand, you're more likely to refresh yourself by doing them during short breaks.

Use successes to praise and replenish yourself. When you complete one micromove, acknowledge it. "Yes, I made the bed for the first time in two weeks." "The statistics for the report are ready a day early." Be as specific as possible and give yourself permission to wallow in praise.

When you fill your own emotional bucket, it's easier to give to others.

Before you start, do the preparation described at the beginning of Part II.

Turn to the PARDA Process

Pause during your day and on weekends. Ask yourself what you're enjoying right now. Or do you always tell yourself you'll make time later? I kept meaning to see a certain art exhibit, but then it left the gallery. I was too late.

Acknowledge what arises, including guilt, for taking "me" time. Are you the kind of person who gives to others but doesn't support yourself? Do you feel resentful at having a lot to do when you see others at ease? Does this entire topic make you squirm? Do you find reasons to avoid the PARDA Process when thinking about play? Why?

Write down your feelings on this topic. Having worked since my early teens and raised by a busy stay-at-home mom and a dad who worked six days a week most of his life, I didn't realize how hard it was for me to accept any free time to unwind.

Reflect on the fact that what helps you unwind may be unappealing to someone else. Depending on your age, a night out dancing in the clubs sounds great, and you don't have to worry about work the next day if it's on a weekend.

If children are involved, do you seek family-friendly options that are low-cost or free? I've discovered a local living history farm about half an hour from my house. It's a delight to explore, no matter the season. I find viewing the animals and enjoying the stillness of the lake a balm to my spirit. I suspect I would not have savored it as much when I was younger.

"Surround yourself with people who take their work seriously, but not themselves, those who work hard and play hard." - Colin Powell

Recall what you enjoyed doing as a child. Now that you're an adult, do you have any wistful daydreams about being a ballerina or an artist? Do you feel embarrassed about your choices or think they're silly? Looking back, did you have time to be you, or were your days filled with classes and after-school activities? Did you choose activities for yourself? Or did well-meaning parents pressure you? When unexpected time appears, do you panic at the lack of structure and use it to get caught up instead of savoring it for your enjoyment?

Decide if you want more "me" time. How much time do you have? What activities sound appealing? After being behind a desk, many people want to get far away. If you work alone all day, then you'll want to be with friends. Do you deal with the public? Then you'll seek quiet pursuits. Whatever your situation, challenge yourself to find moments of pleasure during the day. Take a walk during your lunch hour or work on a craft to unwind.

Act on any realizations you have had regarding the role of pleasure and play in your life. What playful activity will you plan before the week is out? How can you make a regular practice of finding fun?

When you write down an activity, be sure to follow through, honoring your commitment to yourself just as you would to your friends. Again, refer to Appendix C, 101+ Ways to Pause and Savor for suggestions on how to savor life.

Part III Appendices

Appendix A

The Good News of Jesus Christ

When you read this book, you might be annoyed, baffled, or curious about the Scripture references throughout. I include them because I came to God in my need and as a skeptic who became a believer based upon what the Bible says, not how I feel.

I challenge you to "Oh, taste and see that the LORD is good!" Psalm 34:8 (ESV)

While we want to come to God on our terms, we are separated from Him because of our sin and sinful behavior. There is a tension between seeing God as loving but also holy beyond our comprehension. We have chosen to follow our own desires, according to the Scriptures. "For all have sinned, and fall short of the glory of God." Romans 3:23 (NKJV) "All we like sheep have gone astray; we have turned everyone to his own way; and the LORD hath laid on him the iniquity of us all." Isaiah 53:6 (KJV)

God is holy and just, as well as loving. While we want to see God as a loving God (and He is), sin must be acknowledged and paid for. Most of us have experienced a sense of emptiness that nothing satisfies. Augustine of Hippo (354-430) said it well when he wrote in *Confessions*, "Our hearts are restless, until they can find rest in you."

There is nothing we can do or give to God to earn our salvation. Nothing.

"For by grace you have been saved through faith. And this is not your own doing; it is the gift of God, not a result of works, so that no one may boast." Ephesians 2:8-9 (ESV)

"He saved us, not because of works done by us in righteousness, but according to his own mercy, by the washing of regeneration and renewal of the Holy Spirit, whom he poured out on us richly through Jesus Christ our Savior." Titus 3:5-6 (ESV)

"He died for all, that they who live should no longer live for themselves, but for Him who died and rose again on their behalf." II Corinthians 5:15 (NASB)

I challenge you to come to Jesus Christ and acknowledge your need for Him. As II Corinthians 6:2 (ESV) says, "Behold, now is the favorable time; behold, now is the day of salvation."

Accept the fact that you are a sinner and personally believe (trust) in Jesus Christ as the only way to receive forgiveness from God and enter heaven.

"But as many as received Him to them He gave the right to become children of God, even to those who believe in His name." John 1:12 (NASB)

"Whoever believes in the Son has eternal life; whoever does not obey the Son shall not see life, but the wrath of God remains on him." John 3:36 (ESV)

We must confess with our mouth, and believe in our hearts, to be saved.

"...that if you confess with your mouth Jesus as Lord, and believe in your heart that God raised Him from the dead, you shall be saved; for with the heart man believes, resulting in righteousness, and with the mouth he confesses, resulting in salvation." Romans 10:9-10 (NASB)

If you have believed in the Lord Jesus Christ and prayed Romans 10:9-10, know that your salvation is assured. It is not an emotional experience that changes based upon your feelings. "I write these things to you who believe in the name of the Son of God, that you may know that you have eternal life." I John 5:13 (ESV)

"Truly, truly, I say to you, he who hears My word, and believes Him who sent Me, has eternal life, and does not come into judgment, but has passed out of death into life." John 5:24 (NASB)

Appendix B

What to Say When It's All Falling Apart

When you're numb or in shock because of unwelcome news or ongoing stress, what do you say to yourself?

I've used different thoughts to get through rough patches, and made a list. Feel free to use them as is or as jumping-off points to create your own. They include:

Fairy tales start with "And it came to pass," but they don't say, "And it came to stay." The same is true of this trouble in my life.

"I can do all things through Christ who strengtheneth me." (Philippians 4:13, NKJ)

This, too, shall pass. It may take a while, but life doesn't stand still.

What can I control? What must I let go? Who will help me?

How much will this matter five years from now?

We will get through this, so keep calm and carry on.

We've been through tough times before and we will again.

"Life goes on." (Robert Frost)

"Ninety percent of what I worried about never happened." (Mark Twain)

"What do I need to know about this?" (Barbara McNichol)

Appendix C

101+ Ways to Pause and Savor

Everyone asks me how to pause and enjoy the moment. Why this is difficult to do, I'm not sure. But to get you started in a new habit for enjoying life, see this list of actions that engages your senses. Some take seconds to do while others take longer, depending on the time you have available. The prompts are deliberately vague to allow you to decide which senses to engage when you **Pause**.

Do you admire the satiny finish on the cedar chest, or does the smell catch your attention? What feelings and memories arise when you explore your senses?

Feel free to combine and explore the different experiences noted in this list. Better still, discover your own delectable ways to pause and savor. Enjoy.

A crisp apple

Old, gleaming pewter

Different instruments in a symphony

Biting into a piece of your mom's fried chicken

Cheesecake

Smell of sage from the southwestern United States

Sliding into a hot tub

Waves at the lake or seashore

Crunchy salad

Old-fashioned lollipops from your childhood

Poignant notes of "Taps"

Sips of tea or coffee

Chewy taffy

Individual frozen grapes

Open cedar wood chest

Crunchy string beans, raw or cooked

Cookies baking in the oven

Your yard after a summer rain

Flock of geese flying in formation

Scent of your favorite store

Freshly washed and changed infant

Sniffing a puppy or kitten

Rainbows

Salty crackers

Sheets smelling fresh from hanging outside

Raindrops drumming on a sturdy roof

Lavender from your grandmother's sheets or sachets

Motion of your body as you paddle a canoe

Clink of cups and silverware at a favorite coffee shop

Salty air of the New England seashore

Old-fashioned heirloom roses

Carrots fresh from the garden

Clay used in a potter's studio

Turpentine

Brie cheese

Oil paints

English clotted cream

Fresh-cut hay

Walking through a large pile of leaves

Pot of soup simmering on the stove

"New car" smell

Rubbing lotion on dry, chapped skin

Changing colors in a lake or river

Sliding into bed on clean flannel sheets

A mango, the juice dripping down your chin

Rubbing the sleek hide of a horse or cow

Warm bread fresh from the oven

Smell of your favorite relative's perfume

Curved railing of a staircase

Crackling fire

Your bare feet on a hot sidewalk

Rich taste of high-quality chocolate

Rain splashing on your face

Sound of wind chimes in the distance

Texture of your loved one's skin

Running sand through your fingers

Kneading pastry dough

Spicy tortilla soup

Feeling the turns of your car driving on a country road

Handling your favorite piece of jewelry

Listening to bagpipes

A loved one rubbing knots out of your shoulders

Sinking into your favorite chair

Rhythm of your fingers when knitting or crafting

First glimpses of mountains in the distance

Standing under a warm shower before or after work

Gently stroking the feathers of a bird

Running sand through your fingers

Sound of thunder

Your body in motion while exercising

A baby cooing and giggling

Al dente pasta

Door opening as a special someone arrives

Subtle shades of green in farmers' fields

Wrapping up in a quilt when you feel chilly

Your best friend's voice

Cold lemonade on a muggy day

Listening to a variety of regional and local accents

Dancing in sync with your partner

Smell of cutting open a lemon

Call of a loon on a quiet lake

Pine trees in a forest

Deep bass notes of an organ

Subtlety of the grain in a piece of polished wood

Rhythmic music that gets your body moving

Chirping birds at sunrise

Full men's or women's chorus

Stroking the plush of a stuffed animal

Clip-clop of a horse's hoofs

Rustle of leaves

Hushed stillness of a sacred place

Gurgle of your favorite hot beverage being poured

Winter sunset in gold and purple

Your loved one's face before you turn off the lights

Click of your dog's paws through the house

Meteor showers

Fresh pesto

Rows of fresh fruits and vegetables at your market

Rich colors of medieval paintings

Clothes or books arranged in order

Smelling a barnyard filled with cows and horses

Variety of colors in a head of hair or on an animal's fur

Birds swooping and dipping in the wind

Your favorite song on the radio

Billows and shapes of clouds through the seasons

Colors of foliage in the fall

Walking into your home after weeks or months away

Hearing holiday music

Details of a full moon

Array of colors in a yarn shop

Shape of driftwood on a beach

Soaring height of a city skyscraper

Sunlight through a window

Lifting a weighty box

Patterns from moving shadows on the floor

Sensation of movement of a swing

Recommended Resources

Here's a list of helpful books and websites for sorting out your life. Most of the authors listed also have websites and blogs. Rather than listing both, I provide the book titles and suggest searching for the authors online.

While I have enjoyed these books and websites, the opinions and ideas mentioned in them are not necessarily mine. I take no responsibility for how you choose to use the information.

Books

Aarons-Mele, Morra. *Hiding in the Bathroom: An Introvert's Roadmap to Getting Out There (When You'd Rather Stay Home)*. New York: HarperCollins Publishers, 2017.

Bridges, Jerry. *Transforming Grace.* Carol Stream, Illinois: NavPress, division of Tyndale House Publishers, Inc., 2017.

Cepero, Helen. *Journaling as a Spiritual Practice: Encountering God Through Attentive Writing.* Westmont, Illinois: IVP Books, 2008.

Duhigg, Charles. *The Power of Habit: Why We Do What We Do in Life and Business.* New York: Random House Trade Paperbacks, 2014.

McKeown, Greg. *Essentialism: The Disciplined Pursuit of Less.* New York: Crown Business, 2014.

Morgan, Robert J. *The Strength You Need: The Twelve Great Strength Passages of the Bible.* Nashville, Tennessee: W Publishing Group, an imprint of Thomas Nelson, 2016.

Newport, Cal. *Deep Work: Rules for Focused Success in a Distracted World*. New York: Grand Central Publishing, 2016.

Pennebaker, James, and Evans, John. *Expressive Writing: Words that Heal*. Enumclaw, Washington: Idyll Harbor, 2014.

Pillay, Srini. *Tinker Dabble Doodle Try: Unlock the Power of the Unfocused Mind*. New York: Ballantine Books, 2017.

Pychyl, Timothy A. *Solving the Procrastination Puzzle: A Concise Guide to Strategies for Change.* New York, New York: Penguin Publishing Group, 2013.

Selk, Jason. *Organize Tomorrow Today: 8 Ways to Retrain Your Mind to Optimize Performance at Work and in Life.* New York: Da Capo Lifelong Books. Boston, Massachusetts, 2015.

Sterner, Thomas M. *The Practicing Mind: Developing Focus and Discipline in Your Life*. Novato, California: New World Library, 2005, 2012.

Strobel, Lee. *The Case for Christ: A Journalist's Personal Investigation of the Evidence for Jesus*. Grand Rapids, Michigan: Zondervan; Updated, expanded edition, 2016.

Waldman, Mark Robert, and Manning, Chris. *NeuroWisdom: The New Brain Science of Money, Happiness, and Success.* New York: Diversion Publishing Corp., 2017.

Websites

Given the sheer number of websites and resources available, it's easy to get distracted. Listed below are a few sites I've returned to more than once. All sites were available as of January 2018.

www.entrepreneur.com – As its name suggests, this site targets entrepreneurs and small business owners. Still, its content about finance, social media, marketing, and other topics are enjoyable for anyone.

www.flylady.net by Marla Cilley – This hilarious website is loaded with practical suggestions on becoming clean and organized. And no, its founder, Marla Cilley, is not a pilot. She enjoys fly fishing and teaches it at a local college.

www.lifehack.org – This site offers a host of articles on communication, life change, psychology, and more. The home page notes, "Get refreshing ideas to end negativity, get things done fast, and achieve bigger goals."

www.unlockingthebible.org – This site offers the "Gospel-Centered Teaching of Pastor Colin Smith." It contains devotional materials, a blog, and other resources for those wishing to grow in their Christian walk.

https://zenhabits.net by Leo Babauta – This site offers a holistic view of looking at life and suggestions to make it work. Anyone who can live a simple life in San Francisco along with being the father of six children has my admiration.

Acknowledgments

Authors never write books in isolation. If it weren't for family, friends, and professionals, we wouldn't get it done. I am incredibly blessed by the people who support me.

Don and Marianne: Love and hugs for years of love, prayers, and encouragement. You are both an inspiration to me.

Anne, Marikay, and Sharon: Thanks for listening to me rant and rave. Your love, laughter, and prayers have sustained me. Here's to more time, phone calls, and meals.

Barbara McNichol, of Barbara McNichol Editorial: Thank you for shaping this mass of words into a readable book. How did you make me sound better and keep your sense of humor in the process?

Angela Hoy, owner of BookLocker and the entire BookLocker team: Thank you for all your support and making me part of your author family. I am honored.

Leif Jensen, CPA: You pushed me to put my money where my mouth is and make something of my writing. Thank you for your compassion, strength and ongoing encouragement.

Mark Grismanauskas, web developer extraordinaire, thank you for the great web site, and your patience with a WordPress newbie. Let's keep doing breakfast.

Luisa Buehler, my fellow writer and business owner, I'm delighted we connected. Thank you for your kind emails and keep on writing.

Robert Beiter, Ph.D., Audiologist: It's always a pleasure to meet with you and the gang to laugh and figure out ways to help me hear better.

Ann Collins, D.C.: Now you know why there have been so many knots in my back. Your compassion and humor heal as much as your skilled touch.

Patricia Cannon, Ph.D.: You taught me how to do research and enjoy the process. I'm delighted we've stayed in touch.

Carol Solomon, Ph.D., business coach: You heard it first and encouraged me to write it down. Thank you.

To clients, patrons, friends, and strangers who have shared your stories with me: You are the reason the PARDA Process was born and refined.

Most of all, to my husband Ron: You mean the world to me. Words can't express my love and appreciation for your years of love and unwavering support. You never gave up on my dreams when I was down. I am blessed beyond measure to have you as my husband. "Thank you" doesn't begin to express how much I appreciate who you are and what you have meant to me.

Citations

[1] Matthew Hutson, Positive Thinking Leads Economic Decline. *Psychology Today*, posted February 14, 2014, https://www.psychologytoday.com/blog/psyched/201402/positive-thinking-leads-economic-decline, accessed November 5, 2017.

[2] The Pen Is Mightier Than the Keyboard: Advantages of Longhand Over Laptop Note Taking, Psychological Science OnlineFirst, published May 22, 2014 (doi:10.1177/0956797614524581) accessed Nov. 5, 2017.

[3] Susan Payne Carter, Kyle Greenberg and Michael S. Walker, The impact of computer usage on academic performance: Evidence from a randomized trial at the United States Military Academy. *Economics of Education Review*, 2017, vol. 56, issue C, 118-132, accessed November 5, 2017.

[4] http://calnewport.com/blog/2009/10/21/the-hidden-art-of-practice/

[5] Darryl McDaniels with Darrell Dawsey, *Ten Ways Not to Commit Suicide: A Memoir*. HarperCollins, 2016, p. 166.

[6] Timothy D. Wilson, David A. Reinhard, Erin C. Westgate, Daniel T. Gilbert, Nicole Ellerbeck, Cheryl Hahn, Casey L. Brown, Adi Shaked. Just think: The challenges of the disengaged mind. *Science* 04 Jul 2014: Vol. 345, Issue 6192, pp. 75-77. DOI: 10.1126/science.1250830, accessed November 5, 2017.

[7] Chris Woolson, Barista's Burden: The Dark Side of "Service with a Smile." "KnowableMagazine.org," March 3, 2018. https://www.knowablemagazine.org/article/mind/2018/baristas-burden, accessed April 10, 2018.

[8] Antonio Damasio, How Emotion Shapes Decision Making, "The Intentional Workplace," March 15, 2012. https://intentionalworkplace.com/2012/03/15/how-emotion-shapes-decision-making, accessed November 9, 2017.

[9] Lissa Rankin, *The Fear Cure: Cultivating Courage as Medicine for the Body, Mind and Soul.* Hay House, Inc.; 2015.

[10] https://compassionatemind.co.uk/about-us

[11] http://www.compassionfocusedtherapy.com

[12] Kristen Neff, *Self-Compassion: The Proven Power of Being Kind to Yourself.* William Morrow, 2011.

[13] https://bulletproofmusician.com/gain-a-psychological-edge-by-talking-about-yourself-in-the-third-person/, accessed November 8, 2017.

[14] Michala Chung, *The Irresistible Introvert: Harness the Power of Quiet Charisma in a Loud World.* Skyhorse Publishing, 2016.

[15] E. Kross, E. Bruehlman-Senecal, J. Park, Burson, Dougherty, Shablack, Bremner, Moser. Self-talk as a regulatory mechanism: how you do it matters.

Journal of Personality and *Social Psychology*. 2014 Feb;106(2):304-24, accessed November 12, 2017.

16 Jason S. Moser, Adrienne Dougherty, Whitney I. Mattson, Benjamin Katz, Tim P. Moran, Darwin Guevarra, Holly Shablack, Ozlem Ayduk, John Jonides, Marc G. Berman & Ethan Kross. Third-person self-talk facilitates emotion regulation without engaging cognitive control: Converging evidence from ERP and fMRI. *Scientific Reports 7*, Article number: 4519 (2017). Published online 03 July 2017; accessed November 9, 2017.

17 Sheena S. Iyengar, and Mark R. Lepper. When Choice is De-motivating: Can One Desire Too Much of a Good Thing? *Journal of Personality and Social Psychology*. 2000, Dec; 79(6):995-1006, accessed November 18, 2017.

18 Heidi Grant Halvorson, Ph.D., and E. Tory Higgins, Ph.D. *Focus: Use Different Ways of Seeing the World for Success and Influence.* New York: Hudson Street Press, 2013.

19 Sherry Turkle, *Reclaiming Conversation: The Power of Talk in a Digital Age.* New York: Penguin Press, 2015.

20 Barry Schwartz, *The Paradox of Choice: Why More is Less.* New York: Ecco, 2004.

21 Twyla Tharp, *The Creative Habit: Learn It and Use It for Life.* New York: Simon & Schuster, 2003.

22 Gabriele Oettingen, *Rethinking Positive Thinking: Inside the New Science of Motivation.* New York: Penguin Publishing Group, 2014.

23 Kurt Henry Becker, *American "KAIZEN"–A Perspective on American Management Theories.* Utah State University, 1997. Utah State University Digital Commons@USU. EED Faculty Publications, Engineering Education. http://digitalcommons.usu.edu/cgi/viewcontent.cgi?article=1011&context=et e_facpub, accessed November 10, 2017.

24 Betsy Chasse, *Tipping Sacred Cows: The Uplifting Story of Spilt Milk and Finding Your Own Spiritual Path in a Hectic World.* New York: Atria Books/Beyond Words, 2014.

25 Ibid. p. 58.

26 Email received November 17, 2017.

27 James C. Coyne, Ph.D. and Howard Tennen, Ph.D. "Positive Psychology in Cancer Care: Bad Science, Exaggerated Claims and Unproven Medicine." *Annals of Behavioral Medicine*, 2010 Feb; 39(1): 16–26. Published online 2010 Feb 10. (doi: 10.1007/s12160-009-9154-z), accessed November 12, 2017.

28 Barbara Fredrickson, *Positivity: Top-Notch Research Reveals the 3-to-1 Ratio That Will Change Your Life.* Potter/Ten Speed/Harmony, 2009.

29 Barbara L. Fredrickson and Marcial F. Losada, "Positive Affect and the Complex Dynamics of Human Flourishing." *American Psychologist*, 2005 Oct;

60(7): 678–686 (doi: 10.1037/0003-066X.60.7.678), accessed November 12, 2017.

30N. J. L. Brown, A. D. Sokal, & H. L. Friedman, "The Complex Dynamics of Wishful Thinking: The Critical Positivity Ratio." July 15, 2013. Advance online publication. (doi: 10.1037/a0032850)
http://www.physics.nyu.edu/sokal/complex_dynamics_final_clean.pdf

31 http://retractionwatch.com/2013/09/19/fredrickson-losada-positivity-ratio-paper-partially-withdrawn/, accessed November 11, 2017.

32 Barbara Ehrenreich, *Nickel and Dimed: On (not) Getting By in America.* New York: Henry Holt, 2002.

33 Barbara Ehrenreich, *Bright-sided: How Positive Thinking Is Undermining America.* New York: 1st Picador ed., Picador, 2009.

34 A. Timur Sevincer, Greta Wagner, Johanna Kalvelage, and Gabriele Oettingen, "Positive Thinking About the Future in Newspaper Reports and Presidential Addresses Predicts Economic Downturn." *Psychological Science* 2014, Vol. 25(4) 1010 –1017.

35 Bette Liu, D.Phil., Sarah Floud, Ph.D., Kirstin Pirie, M.Sc., Prof. Jane Green, D.Phil., Prof. Richard Peto, F.R.S., Prof. Valerie Beral, F.R.S. for the Million Women Study Collaborators, "Does happiness itself directly affect mortality? The prospective UK Million Women Study." *The Lancet*, Volume 387, No. 10021, pp. 874–881, 27 February 2016.
http://www.thelancet.com/journals/lancet/article/, accessed November 17, 2017.

36 Susan David, *Emotional Agility: Get Unstuck, Embrace Change and Thrive in Work and Life.* New York: Avery Publishing, 2016.

37 Peter Dunn, "Pete the Planner: Financial life is all about behavior." *IndyStar*, September 14, 2016.

38 Semega, Jessica L., Kayla R. Fontenot, and Melissa A. Kollar: U.S. Census Bureau. *Current Population Reports, p. 60-259, Income and Poverty in the United States: 2016.* U.S. Government Printing Office, Washington, DC, 2017. Accessed January 12, 2018.

39 Harvard Finds That Medical Bills Push Many into Bankruptcy. *Harvard Law Today*, February 3, 2005. https://today.law.harvard.edu/harvard-study-finds-medical-bills-push-many-into-bankruptcy/, accessed November 12, 2017.

40 https://www.nerdwallet.com/blog/average-credit-card-debt-household, accessed November 12, 2017.